Synonyms & Antonyms

Shabnam Gupta

4735/22, Prakash Deep Building
Ansari Road, Darya Ganj,
New Delhi - 110002

Lotus Press : Publishers & Distributors
Unit No. 220, 2nd Floor, 4735/22, Prakash Deep Building,
Ansari Road, Darya Ganj, New Delhi- 110002
Ph.: 23280047, 98118-38000
• E-mail : lotuspress1984@gmail.com
www.lotuspress.co.in

Synonyms & Antonyms

ISBN: 81-89093-89-4

Printed & Published by : **Lotus Press Publisher & Distributors,** New Delhi-02

Synonyms & Antonyms

Published by :
Lotus Press Publishers & Distributors

CONTENTS

FROM THE AUTHOR'S DESK

Having been a student of English Literature, I have always been fascinated with words and their usage. It is the unique interplay of words which can either strengthen or weaken our expression. While reading the books of famous novelists, what interested me the most was how they were able to weave a picture just with the help of words. These words are important tools, and I thought that a handbook which lists both synonyms and antonyms of a word in one place, without the needless turning of pages, would come in most handy. The compiling and editing of this book has been as interesting as it was painstaking. I hope my readers enjoy referring to this book as much as I enjoyed compiling it.

PREFACE

English is inarguably one of the richest, most well - endowed of all the languages in the world. It has the largest vocabulary and the most synonyms of all the languages known to man. It has grown over centuries, and is perhaps the only language which has absorbed words from other languages as well. It has such a diverse character that the same word can have a totally opposite meaning depending on the context in which it is used.

A Synonym is a word which has an identical, similar or equivalent meaning. An exact meaning of a word cannot exist; it will vary with the context in which it is being used. For good English speaking and/or writing, it is important to know the meaning as well as the usage.

An Antonym is a word that is opposite in meaning. Just like it is not possible to have an exact synonym, it is also not possible to have an exact antonym. So, an approximate one has to be known. Also, not all words have an antonym. Here, you'll find the synonyms and the antonyms of a word in one place.

This book has been written as an aid for students of English to help them to communicate more effectively. Linguistic scholars point out that words change in meaning according to time, place and circumstance. With all the changes that are going on in the literary world, and the inclusion of words from other languages, it is difficult to have one internationally standardized book on this subject. This book has been written specifically keeping the contemporary Indian reader in mind.

A

Abandon (verb)

syn – relinquish, drop, adjure, quit, forsake, leave, retire from, surrender, resign, forego, yield, vacate, waive, desert, cast off.

ant – restraint , retain

Abase (verb)

syn – degrade, demean, humble, humiliate, mortify.

ant – regard, commend.

Abash (verb)

syn – chagrin, confuse, discomfit, discomfort, embarrass, faze, mortify, discountenance.

Abate(verb)

syn – decrease, diminish, drain, dwindle, ebb, lessen, let up, deduct, discount, rebate, lapse, remit, subside, fall, moderate, wane.

ant – increase, rise.

Abbreviate (verb)

syn – abridge, condense, curtail, reduce, shorten.

ant – lengthen, elongate.

Abduct (verb)

syn – kidnap, snatch, spirit away.

Aberration (noun)

syn – abnormality, deviation, anomaly, deviance, irregularity, unnaturalness.

ant – conformity, usual.

Abet (verb)

syn – aid, assist, boost, relieve, succor, help out.

ant – hinder, obstruct.

Abeyance (noun)

syn – intermission, latency, suspension, quiescence, dormancy.

ant – apparent, present.

Abhor (verb)

syn – hate, detest, loathe, disgust , abominate , shrink from , recoil , shudder with horror.

ant – adore, love, admire

Abide (verb)

syn – stay, reside, continue, remain, dwell, live, inhabit, settle, sojourn, persist, persevere, be constant, tolerate, endure, last, permanent, await, attend, suffer, put up with, sustain.

ant – break, change.

Abjure (verb)

syn – disavow, recall, retract, withdraw, recant.

ant – accept.

Able (adjective)

syn – capable, competent, good, skilled, skillful.

ant – disable.

Abnormal (adjective)

syn – aberrant, anomalistic, atypical, deviant, divergent, unnatural, irregular.

ant – normal, good.

Abominable(adjective)

syn – abhorrent, filthy, foul, contemptible, despicable, rotten, repugnant, lousy, infamous, odious, low, vile, wretched, detestable, disgusting, obnoxious.

ant – adorable, admirable.

Abound (verb)

syn – bristle, crawl, flow, overflow, swarm, teem.

ant – scarcity, absence.

Abrogate (verb)

syn – negate, nullify, vitiate, cancel, annul, abolish, annihilate, invalidate, void.

ant – continue.

Abrupt (adjective)

syn – hurried, blunt, brief, sudden, precipitate, brusque, curt, gruff, bold, cut short, sheer, steep.

Absolute(adjective)

syn – autocratic, despotic, tyrannical, totalitarian, dictatorial, implicit, undoubting, unfaltering, unreserved, wholehearted, perfect, unflawed, unconditional, perfect, plain, pure, simple, unadulterated, undiluted, unreserved, unqualified, impeccable, complete, outright, thorough, total, unlimited, unmitigated.

ant – limited.

Absorb (verb)

syn – assimilate, digest, imbibe, incorporate , ingest, receive, gather, acquire, gain, get, pick up.

ant – disgorge, disperse, dissipate, eject, emit , exude.

Absurd (adjective)

syn – farcical, foolish, ludicrous, silly, senseless, unreasonable, preposterous, irrational, fantastic, contrary to common sense.

ant – consistent, logical, rational, reasonable, sagaci - ous.

Abundance (noun)

syn – mass, plenty, profusion, heap, pack, pile, plentitude, bountifulness, wealth, much.

ant – want, deficiency, scarcity.

Abysmal (adjective)

syn – cavernous, gaping, yawning, wide open.

ant – closed.

Accentuate(verb)

Syn – accent, stress, underline, underscore, emphasize, feature, highlight.

ant – underplay, downplay.

Accept (verb)

syn – admit, receive, embrace, accede, agree, assent, consent, subscribe, believe, abide, bear, suffer, sustain, tolerate, withstand, have, take, apprehend, fathom, get, grasp, read, sense, see.

ant – reject, negate, contra dict.

Access (noun)

syn – admittance, entrance, entry, ingress.

ant – debar, obstruct, hinder.

Accessory (noun/adjective)

syn – accomplice, confederate, conspirator, adjunct, appendage, appurtenance, ancillary, collateral, supportive, subsidiary, auxiliary.

Acclimatize (verb)

syn – accommodate, adapt, adjust, conform, fashion, fit, reconcile, suit, tailor, harden, season, toughen.

Accompany (verb)

syn – attend, chaperon, conduct, convoy, escort, follow, consort, keep company with, go along, go hand in hand with.

ant – leave, desert.

Accomplice (noun)

syn – abettor, accessory, conspirator, plotter, partner in crime or wrong doing.

ant – opponent, rival, competitor.

Accord (noun/verb)

syn – agreement, arrangement, deal, pact, understanding, rapport, harmony, tune, unity, concert, tune, convention, treaty, agree, check, consist, correspond, award, bestow, confer, grant, concede, vouchsafe.

ant – discord.

Accredit (verb)

syn – ascribe, assign, attribute, charge, credit, impute, authorize, entitle, license, qualify.

Accrue (verb)

syn – aggregate, amass, collect, garner, gather, hive, pile up, accumulate.

ant – diminish, dwindle.

Accumulate (verb)

syn – amass, collect, gather, hoard, pile, amass, aggregate, gather up, leap up, scrape together, store, accrue, treasure up, set by, increase, grow.

ant – disperse, dissipate, scatter, spend, squander, waste.

Accurate (adjective)

syn – correct, exact, nice, precise, right, true, unerring, flawless, factual .

ant – inaccurate, incorrect, approximate.

Accuse (verb)

syn – arraign, charge, impeach, incriminate, indict, blame, censure .

ant – exonerate, pardon, forgive.

Accustom (verb)

syn – condition, habituate, inure, wont.

Acerbic (adjective)

syn – acid, caustic, mordacious, mordant, pungent, scathing, trenchant, bitter, harsh, sour, tangy, truculent, vitriolic, corrosive, biting.

ant – sweet, sugary.

Acknowledge (verb)

syn – admit, concede, confess, own, validate, recognize, be aware of, allow, endorse, subscribe to, grant, own, profess.

ant – forswear, contradict.

Acme (noun)

syn – summit, top, apex, climax, highest point, zenith, peak, pinnacle, culmination.

ant – base, bottom, foot, nadir.

Acquaint (verb)

syn – introduce, advise, apprise, educate, enlighten, inform, notify.

Action (noun)

syn – movement, deed, feat, operation, exploit, motion, play, performance, force, energy, process, prosecution, battle, encounter, combat, bustle, commotion, stir, to-do.

ant – inaction, inertia, sloth.

Actual (adjective)

syn – real, true, existent, extant, authentic, genuine, indubitable, original, undoubted, unquestionable.

ant – fictitious, spurious.

Acumen (adjective)

syn – acuity, insight, perception, shrewdness, ingenuity, penetration, discernment, sharpness.

ant – bluntness, obtuseness, dullness, stupidity.

Acute (adjective)

syn – keen, severe, violent, intense, sharp, pointed, penetrating, high, shrill.

ant – bland, languid, slow, stupid.

Adamant (adjectivc)

syn – implacable, inflexible, obdurate, relentless, rigid, stubborn, unbending, unrelenting, unyielding.

ant – flexible, yielding.

Adapt (verb)

syn – accommodate, adjust, suit, qualify, prepare, co-ordinate, match, conform, square, make, reconcile, yield.

ant – Derange, discompose, disjoin, dislocate, dissent, resist.

Addle (verb)

syn – befuddle, bewilder, jumble, muddle, confuse,

mystify, perplex, puzzle, dizzy.

ant – enlighten, clarify.

Addition (noun)

syn – Affix, annex, appendage, attach, accessory, adjunct, appendix, supplement, sum, join, connection, aggregate, count up, appurtenance.

ant – subtraction, deletion, omission.

Address (verb/noun)

syn – direct, accost, speak to, apply to, court, salute, invoke, appeal, request, entreaty., application, speech, lecture, oration, skill, sermon.

ant – ignore.

Adept (noun/adjective)

syn – expert, master, proficient, skillful, authority.

ant – inexpert, inexperienced.

Adequate (adjective)

syn – enough, sufficient, satisfactory.

ant – inadequate, deficient, insufficient.

Adhere (verb)

syn – cling, hold, stick, belong, stand by, cleave, be firmly fixed, devoted to, be true.

ant – leave, separate, sever.

Adjourn (verb)

syn – defer, delay, hold off, remit, shelve, suspend, waive.

Adjunct (noun)

syn – accessory, appurtenance, supplement, attachment, appendage.

Advance (verb/noun)

syn – push, promote, exalt, dignify, set forward, propel, shone, raise to higher rank, improve, make better, increase, enhance, proceed, get forward, rise, march, prosper, thrive, tender, proffer, rise, appreciation.

ant – delay, hinder, sidetrack, cease.

Adversity (noun)

syn – disaster, trouble, suffering, affliction, calamity, misfortune, hard times, bad luck.

ant – fortune, favourable, compatibility.

Advice (noun)

syn – counsel, recommendation, suggestion, purpose, tidings, information, warning, forethought.

ant – misinform.

Afraid (adjective)

syn – alarmed, anxious, aghast, fearful, scared, apprehensive, frightened, terror-stricken.

ant – audacious, brave, calm, confident.

Affront (verb/noun)

syn – insult, offend, abuse, anger, gall, outrage, displease, provoke, vex, annoy, give displeasure, smite.

ant – praise, pacify.

After (preposition)

syn – subsequent, following, behind, later, rear, imitation, on model of, afterwards, back.

ant – before.

Alcoholic (noun)

syn – boozer, drunk, drunkard, inebriate, tippler, wino, dipsomaniac, sot.

ant – sober, abstainer, teetotaler.

Alien (adjective)

syn – foreign, not native, remote, estranged, strange, inappropriate, separated, unallied, irrelevant.

ant – native, indigenous.

Allay (verb)

syn – repress, smoothen, lull, still, quieten, check, subdue, appease, pacify, compose, assuage, calm, soften, mitigate, lessen, ease, dull, palliate, blunt, mollify.

ant – aggravate

Allegiance (noun)

syn – fidelity, loyalty, fealty, trust, commitment.

ant – disloyalty, treachery, treason, sedition, rebellion.

Allure (verb)

syn – tempt, seduce, decoy, troll, lure, invite, attract, entice, beguile, solicit, win over, coax , cajole, engage, prevail, upon, inveigle.

ant – disenchant, repel.

Alonc (adjective)

syn – single, solitary, only, lonely, isolated, deserted, sole, by oneself.

ant – together, company.

Altercation (noun)

syn – dispute, fight, controversy, strife, difference of opinion, contention, rupture, quarrel, wrangle, sparring.

ant – amity, peace, agreement, concurrence.

Amalgamation (noun)

syn – mixture, compound, blending, mingling, union, conjunction.

ant – separation.

Amateur (noun)

syn – dabbler, smatterer, uninitiate, nonprofessional, dilettante.

ant – experienced, expert, seasoned.

Amaze (verb)

syn – confound, astound, astonish, stupefy, surprise, dumbfound, confuse, perplex, daze, bewilder.

ant – imperturb .

Ambassador (noun)

syn – envoy, minister, legate, plenipotentiary.

Ambiguity (noun)

syn – doubt, uncertainty, vagueness, obscurity.

ant – clarity, precision.

Ambit (noun)

syn – circuit, compass, perimeter, circumference, periphery, extension, extent, purview, scope, sphere.

Amble (verb)

syn – walk slowly, slow pace, dawdle.

ant – hurry, brisk, walk.

Amenable (adjective)

syn – accountable, liable, responsible, answerable, accepting, docile, obedient, supple, compliant, receptive, open-minded.

ant – stubborn, opinionated, recalcitrant.

Amiss (adjective/adverb)

syn – astray, awry, sour, wrong, afield.

Amnesty (noun)

syn – forgiveness, general pardon.

ant – condemnation.

Amorphous (adjective)

syn – shapeless, formless, structure less, vague, confused, misshapen.

ant – ordered, shapely, organized.

Anathema (noun)

syn – curse, damnation, execration, malediction, abhorrence, aversion, detestation, hate, malediction.

ant – admiration, adoration.

Ancestor (noun)

syn – forbear, forefather, progenitor.

ant – descendant, posterity, offspring, progeny.

Ancient (adjective)

syn – antiquated, old, primitive, obsolete, antique, archaic, of by gone era.

ant – modern, fresh, new, novel, recent.

Anger (verb/noun)

syn – fury, ire, rage, indignation, wrath, bad, temper, gall, exasperation, displease, irritate, provoke, offend, vex, nettle, enrage, inflame, madden, rouse.

ant – clemency, placidity, forbearance, calmness.

Angst (noun)

syn – anxiety, care, concern, disquiet, distress, nervousness, solicitude, unease, worry.

Animosity (noun)

syn – bitterness, rancor, hatred, enmity, malignity, virulence, grudge, ill-will, spleen, hostility.

ant – love, affection, adoration.

Annoy (verb)

syn – bait, beset, harass, pester, plague, tease, torment, worry, peeve, nettle, provoke, exasperate, rile, ruffle, vex, irk, irritate, gall, fret, aggravate, bother, bug, chafe, disturb.

ant – please.

Answer (verb)

syn – reply, respond, retort, correspond, be like, similar, do, be enough, refute, rebut, satisfy, fulfill, suitable to, be responsible or accountable, rejoiner, riposte.

ant – question.

Antagonist (noun)

syn – opponent, rival, enemy, foe, competitor, adversary.

ant – ally, accomplice, associate.

Anxiety (noun)

syn – apprehension, angst, disquiet, dread, worry, foreboding, misgiving, uneasiness.

ant – equanimity, confidence, composure, nonchalance.

Apathy (noun)

syn – dullness, coldness, unconcern, inertness, indifference.

ant – enthusiasm, concern.

Aphorism (noun)

syn – adage, saying, dictum, proverb, maxim, sententious, precept.

Apology (noun)

syn – excuse, plea, justification, vindication, reparation, defence, explanation.

ant – accusation.

Appal (verb)

syn – terrify, frighten, dismay, daunt, horrify, shock, terror, awe.

ant – reassure.

Apparent (adjective)

syn – visible, perceptible, manifest, obvious, open, evident, seeming, legible, unmistakable, in clear sight, ostensible, not real.

ant – hidden, actual.

Appear (verb)

syn – emerge, seem, arise, occur, offer, open, loom, visible, be present in court, manifest, look, show.

ant – disappear, invisible.

Appease (verb)

syn – reconcile, placate, pacify, calm, allay, assuage, mollify, blunt, abate, ease, still, dull, quell, lessen, satisfy, lull, hush.

ant – aggravate, enrage, infuriate.

Appetite (noun)

syn – hunger, desire, craving, hankering, lust, liking, zest, gusto, relish, stomach.

ant – indifference.

Applause (verb)

syn – acclaim, plaudit, acclamation, approval.

ant – reproof, abuse, jeering, censure, vituperation.

Apposite (adjective)

syn – apt, relevant, fit, pertinent, befitting, suitable, seasonable, germane, apropos.

ant – inappropriate, inapt, unfit.

Approximately (adjective)

syn – about, around, roughly, almost, exact,

nearly, accurate.

ant – accurately, precisely.

Aptness (noun)

syn – pertinence, suitableness, appropriateness, expertness, adroitness, tact.

ant – unsuitableness, tactless, inexpertness.

Arbitrary (adjective)

syn – despotic, autocratic, tyrannical, imperious, irresponsible, capricious, wilful, fanciful, whimsical.

ant – reasoned, democratic, logical.

Ardent (adjective)

syn – fury, warm, passionate, burning, fervent, eager, intense, keen, sharp, fierce, earnest, glowing, zealous, devoted, sanguine.

ant – tepid, insipid, cool.

Area (noun)

syn – region, field, tract, domain, circuit, range, sphere, territory, district, surface, expanse.

Argot (noun)

syn – cant, dialect, jargon, lingo, vernacular, lexicon, language.

Argue (verb)

syn – debate, discuss, dispute, reason, exchange of words, dissent.

ant – consent, concur.

Aristocratic (adjective)

syn – noble, high - bred, princely, genteel, titled, of high rank, privileged, belonging to the aristocracy.

ant – plebeian, low born, vulgar, bourgeois.

Arise (verb)

syn – emanate, emerge, issue, move upwards, originate, result, stem, raise, stir-up, wake up, awaken.

ant – asleep, end , sink.

Arrest (verb/noun)

syn – stay, stop, seize, take, capture, apprehend, interrupt, obstruct, hinder, detain, delay, keep back, take into custody, occupy, rivet.

ant – release, stimulate.

Arms (noun)

syn – armament, weapon, arsenal, deterrent, ordnance, embrace, branch, division, prepare, equip.

Artificial (adjective)

syn – imitation, false, synthetic, not real, contrived, impure, affected.

ant – genuine, natural.

Artisan (noun)

syn – skilled worker, designer, creator, craftsman, artificer.

Artistic (adjective)

syn – skilful, aesthetic, arty, mannered, stylized, tasteful, elegant, knowledge of art, harmonious.

ant – displeasing, gaudy, shoddy, tasteless, unaesthetic.

Ascetic (adjective)

syn – austere, abstemious, rigid, puritan, self - denying, denunciatory, abstinent.

ant – lax, lenient, luxurious, carnal.

Askew (adverb)

syn – awry, crooked, twisted, oblique, askance, to one side.

ant – straight.

Aspect (noun)

syn – air, look, bearing, angle, prospect, position, appearance, phase, attitude, direction, outlook.

Assail (verb)

syn – assault, invade, attack, set upon, ply, pelt, storm , malign.

ant – resist, vindicate.

Assert (verb)

syn – affirm, allege, aver, testify, asseverate, avouch, avow, maintain.

ant – contradict, demur, dispute, refute.

Assiduous (adjective)

syn – industrious, diligent, active, busy, devoted, careful, laborious, zealous, persevering, persistent, tireless, painstaking.

ant – indolent, lazy.

Assist (verb)

syn – help, aid, support, aid, relieve, patronise, promote, back, cooperate.

ant – hinder.

Associate (noun)

syn – affiliate, ally, colleague, co-worker, fellow, partner, confidante, accomplice, friend, assistant.

ant – dissociate, enemy, opponent.

Assure (verb)

syn – ensure, promise, guarantee, pledge, declare, vouch, vow, promise solemnly, warrant.

ant – imperil, jeopardize, warn.

Atrocious (adjective)

syn – hideous, flagrant, outrageous, heinous, nefarious, dibolical, monstrous, infernal, hellish.

ant – noble, excellent.

Atrophy (noun/verb)

syn – decadence, decline, degeneration, descend, retrograde, sink, worsen.

ant – incline, rise.

Attach (verb)

syn – affix, annex, append, clip, connect, couple, fasten, fix, moor, secure.

ant – detach, dissociate, sever.

Attack (verb)

syn – assail, invade, encounter, assault, bombard, beseige, charge, storm, aggression, impugn, malign, censure, criticise, raid, onslaught.

ant – aid, protect, uphold.

Attain (verb)

syn – accomplish, achieve, gain, reach, realize, arrive at.

ant – relinquish, discard.

Attend (verb)

syn – accompany, serve, guard, watch, escort, follow, frequent, listen, hear, pay heed, tend, serve, wait, minister.

ant – desert, ignore.

Attempt (noun, verb)

syn – aggression, assault, offense, onset, onslaught, strike, crack, effort, endeavour, go, offer, trial, assay, stab, onrush, seek, strive.

Attest (verb)

syn – certify, testify, vouch, authenticate, confirm, corroborate, evidence, justify, indicate, mark, verify, argue, substantiate, depose.

Attract (verb)

syn – draw, charm, entice, tempt, decoy, enamour, captivate, endear, fascinate, pull, engage.

ant – antagonise, repel.

Attribute (verb/noun)

syn – ascribe, assign, credit, impute, refer, quality, peculiarity, characteristic, property.

ant – deny, separate, dissociate.

Attune (verb)

syn – adjust, fix, regulate, set, accommodate, conform, coordinate, harmonize, integrate, proportion, reconcile.

ant – discordant.

Audacity (noun)

syn – daring, impudence, boldness, insolence, presumptuousness, effrontery, impertinence, sauciness.

ant – timidity, meekness, modesty.

Augur (noun/verb)

syn – diviner, seer, soothsayer, prophet, bode, presage, prognosticate, predict, foretell, soothsay, portend.

Auspicious (adjective)

syn – benign, bright, brilliant, fair, favourable, fortunate, propitious, prosperous, timely, opportune.

ant – inauspicious, unlucky, unfortunate.

Authoritarian (noun)

syn – autocratic, despotic, dictatorial, fascist, oligarchic, tyrannical, paternalistic, plutocratic, totalitarian.

ant – democratic, lenient, lax.

Authentic (adjective)

syn – real, genuine, pure, unadulterated, true, trustworthy, reliable, uncorrupted.

ant – spurious, adulterated, superficial.

Autocrat (noun)

syn – dictator, tyrant, totalitarian, authoritarian, despot.

ant – democrat, benevolent.

Auxiliary (adjective)

syn – ancillary, contributory, secondary, subsidiary.

ant – opponent, essential.

Avail (noun, verb)

syn – benefit, blessing, boon, favor, gain, profit, account, use, utility, serve.

Aver (verb)

syn – affirm, allege, argue, assert, asseverate, avouch, avow, claim, contend, declare, hold, maintain, say, state.

Aversion (noun)

syn – abhorrence, abomination, detestation, hate, anathema, antipathy, horror, loathing, repugnance, revulsion.

ant – admiration, adoration.

Avoid (verb)

syn – elude, shun, evade, escape, eschew, dodge, forbear, keep away from .

ant – catch, solicit, encounter.

Award (verb)

syn – Bounty, honor, premium, prize.

ant – forfeit, penalty.

Aware (adjective)

syn – cognizant, conscious, mindful, on to, informed, having, knowledge.

ant – ignorant, unaware, heedless.

Awash (adjective)

syn – big, brimming, overflowing.

Awe (noun/verb)

syn – dread, fear, reverence, intimidate, daunt, veneration, abashment, wonder.

ant – contempt, disregard.

Awful (adjective/adverb)

syn – appalling, horrible, horrendous, dreadful, fearful, frightful, shocking, terrible, greatly, highly, most, notably, extremely, very.

ant – appealing, pleasing.

Awkward (adjective)

syn – uncouth, clumsy, bungling, inept, maladroit, unrefined, gauche, ungainly, rustic, boorish, gawky, slouching, coarse, loutish.

ant – dexterous, elegant, sophisticated, refined.

Awry (adjective/adverb)

syn – amiss, sour, wrong, astray, afield.

ant – usual, correct.

Axiom (noun)

syn – truism, principle, self-evident and assumed truth.

Ax (noun/verb)

syn – discharge, dismissal, termination, cashier, release, terminate, boot, sack.

ant – retain, keep.

Azure (adjective/noun)

syn – sky colored blue , sky, heaven , blue, expanse, the cerulean vault.

B 

Babble (verb/noun)

syn – jabber, chatter, prattle, chat, gossip, tattle, small talk, idle chat, drivel.

ant – quiet.

Back (noun/verb/adjective/adverb)

syn – backtrack, retreat, retrocede, retrograde, rear, buttress, attest, corroborate, substantiate, confirm, validate, advocate, endorse, recommend, support, uphold, backwards, removed, secluded, solitary, about, around, lonesome, obscure.

ant – front, precede.

Backblocks (noun)

syn – bush, inland, midlands, interior, outback.

ant – city, urban.

Backward (adjective)

syn – depressed, emergent, primitive, underdeveloped, developing.

ant – forward, advanced.

Bad (adjective)

syn – evil, disagreeable, distasteful, objectionable, unpleasant, noxious, hurtful, unwholesome, depraved, corrupt, immoral, sinful, unfair, naughty, unfortunate, miserable, vile, mean, sorry, poor, untoward, serious, unhappy, abominable, incompetent, inferior, regretful.

ant – good, virtuous, well-behaved, desirable.

Badger (verb)

syn – bait, heckle, hector, hound, taunt, bedevil, beleaguer, beset, needle, rile, harass, harry, pester, plague, solicit, beseige.

Badinage (noun)

syn – banter, chaff, raillery, taunt, ribbing, jest.

Bag (noun/verb)

syn – container, large quantity, secured, assured.

Balanced (adjective)

syn – even, commonsensical, prudent, rational, regular, reasonable, sagacious, congruous, harmonious, symmetric, proportionate, sane, sapient, well-grounded.

ant – imbalanced, biased.

Balm (verb)

syn – allay, lull, quiet, settle, still, tranquilize.

ant – wound, aggravate.

Ban (noun/verb)

syn – disallowance, taboo, inhibition, prohibition, enjoin, forbid, interdict, proscribe.

Banal (adjective)

syn – inane, insipid, fatuous, vapid, monotonous, sentimental, superficial, trite, truism, trivial.

ant – original, genuine, meaningful.

Banal (adjective)

syn – hackneyed, stale, tired, commonplace, overworked, trite, stereotypical.

ant – unusual, extraordinary.

Bandy (verb)

syn – discuss, moot, thrash out, exchange, talk over.

ant – silent, reticent.

Bane (noun)

syn – affliction, curse, evil, ill, woe, scourge, plague, destruction, downfall, devastation, havoc, ruin, wreck, canker, contagion, poison.

ant – boon, blessing.

Banish (verb)

syn – deport, exile, expatriate, expel, ostracize, cast out, dismiss, dispel.

ant – welcome, invite.

Balderdash (noun)

syn – rant, bombast, verbiage, froth, chatter, fudge, senselessness, nonsense, gibberish, jargon, drivel, idle talk.

ant – wisdom.

Bar (noun/verb)

syn – cabaret, cocktail, lounge, discotheque, nightclub, saloon, barrier, obstruction, piece of solid material, stripe, band, forum, tribunal, fasten, shut, practicing barrister.

ant – aid, allow, permit.

Barbaric (adjective)

syn – churlish, coarse, crude, crass, gross, ill-bred, primitive, vulgar, uncouth, savage, uncultured, uncivilized, wild.

ant – civilized, polished, refined.

Baronial (adjective)

syn – august, grand, imposing, lordly, noble, regal, royal, splendid, sublime, superb, magnificent.

ant – crass, coarse, vulgar.

Bashful (adjective)

syn – backward, coy, demure, diffident, modest, retiring, shy, timid, shy.

ant – brazen, bold.

Banter (verb/noun)

syn – ridicule, mock, jeer, twit, deride, joke, chaff, raillery, persiflage, badinage, jest.

ant – conversation, discourse, lecture.

Bargain (noun/verb)

syn – sell, convey, contract, convention, stipulation, covenant, purchase, treaty, transaction,

Barter (noun/verb)

syn – exchange, swap, trade.

Basic (noun)

syn – absolute, categorical, fundamental, ultimate, unlimited, groundwork, lowest part, bottom, kernel, specific.

ant – marginal, tangent, provisional, peripheral.

Battle (noun/verb)

syn – fight, war, action, struggle, combat, conflict, contest, brush, collision, skirmish.

ant – peace, treaty, inaction, inertia.

Bawdry (noun)

syn – dirt, filth, obscenity, profanity, ribaldry, smut, vulgarity.

ant – decent, noble.

Bear (verb/adjective)

syn – rough, coarse, savage, impolite, uncivil, boorish, uphold, defend, support, maintain, fortitude, confirm.

ant – drop, resist, discard.

Beast (adjective)

syn – brute, inhuman, coarse, repulsive, vile, filthy, abominable, loathsome.

ant – human.

Beat (verb, adjective)

syn – hit, strike, stir, mix, defeat, hammered out, flagellate, flog, scourge, spank, thrash, whip, assault, regular pulse, rhythm.

ant – caress, fondle.

Beautiful (adjective)

syn – desirable, cute, comely, good-looking, pretty, handsome, gorgeous, charming, pleasing,

ant – ugly, uncomely.

Becoming (adjective)

syn – fit, suitable, adequate, appropriate, proper, seemly, graceful, neat, decorous.

ant – unbecoming.

Begin (verb)

syn – commence, start, onset, launch, inaugurate, imitate, institute, arise, commence, beginning, create, origin.

ant – end, finish, stop.

Behaviour (noun)

syn – conduct, demeanor, manners, deportment, act.

Beleaguer (verb)

syn – besiege, surround, bait, heckle, hector, hound, ride, intimidate.

ant – encourage.

Believe (verb)

syn – faith, credit, confidence, credence, think, fancy, be of the opinion of, entertain, adhere.

ant – disbelieve, suspect, doubt.

Belittle (verb)

syn – deprecate, minimize, discredit, detract, disparage, disapprove, depreciate.

ant – exaggerate, enhance, encourage, extol.

Belligerent (adjective)

syn – aggressive, hostile, offensive, bellicose, unfriendly, vindictive.

ant – cordial, warm, friendly.

Bend (verb)

syn – bow, lean, stoop, turn, twist, step down, be flexible.

ant – rise, straighten, resist.

Beneficial (adjective)

syn – good, healthful, advantageous, profitable, healthy, salutary, wholesome, salubrious, favourable, gainful.

ant – harmful, detrimental, injurious, ruinous.

Benevolence (adjective)

syn – altruism, generosity, unselfishness, charitable, benignant, liberalness goodwill, kindness, philanthropy, humanness.

ant – egoism, malice, malevolence.

Benign (adjective)

syn – beneficent, gracious, obliging, kind, gentle, harmless, favourable, wholesome, kindly, amiable, tender - hearted.

ant – malignant, unfavorable.

Between (preposition/adverb)

syn – amid, amidst, betwixt, among, amongst, in confidence, difference, sharing.

Bewail (verb)

syn – moan, lament, grieve, rue, mourn, express sorrow or grief.

ant – rejoice, celebrate.

Biased (adjective)

syn – one sided, partial, partisan, prejudiced, slanted, subjective, inclined, leaning, predisposed, influenced, bent.

ant – impartial, fair, unprejudiced.

Bidding (noun)

syn – offer, proposal, decree, appointment, mandate, command, order, dictate, behest, precept, injunction, bid.

ant – forbid.

Bigotry (adjective)

syn – bias, intolerance, narrow -mindedness, prejudice, favoritism.

ant – tolerance, impartiality, objectivity.

Bilge (noun)

syn – balderdash, nonsense, trash, drivel, twaddle, poppycock, rigmarole, idiocy, rubbish, blather.

ant – rational, commonsense.

Binge (noun)

syn – carousal, drunk, spree, booze, jag, rampage.

ant – abstinence, restraint.

Bisexual (adjective/noun)

syn – androgynous, epicene, hermaphrodite.

Bitterness (adjective)

syn– acerbity, acrimony, asperity, harshness, sourness, pique, sting, sarcasm, caustic, vindictive.

ant – blandness, sweetness, mildness.

Bizarre (adjective)

syn – fantastic, far-out, grotesque, way- out, outlandish, weird, unbelievable, queer, unusual, exceptional, far-out.

ant – normal, run-of-the-mill.

Blab (verb)

syn – betray, divulge, let out, prattle, idle-chatter, tell tales, disclose, reveal, blabber.

ant – reticence.

Blame (verb/noun)

syn – censure, disapprove, reprehend, accuse, reproach, dispraise, condemn, fault, demerit.

ant – praise, vindicate, approve.

Bland (adjective)

syn – dull, gentle, mild, moderate, soothing, monotonous, tranquil, low key.

ant – exciting, harsh, keen.

Blank (adjective)

syn – bare, clear, empty, vacant, void, deadpan, expressionless, inexpressive, inane, vacuous.

ant – filled, expressive.

Blatant (adjective)

syn – offensive, assertive, noisy, bellowing, clamorous, vociferous.

ant – concealed, reserved, quiet.

Blaze (noun/verb)

syn – flame, light, flare, flash, blazon, make known, publish, proclaim.

ant – conceal, vanquish.

Bleak (adjective)

syn – barren, gaunt, haggard, desolate, wasted, inhospitable, dismal, gloomy.

ant – cheerful, warm, hospitable.

Blend (verb)

syn – combine, mix, mingle, coalesce, unite, fuse, amalgamate.

ant – separate, clash, conflict.

Blind (adjective/verb/noun)

syn – sightless, unseeing, ignorant, undiscerning, injudicious, incapable of judging, obscure, dim, labyrinthine, dark, heedless, careless, rash, darkness, hoodwink, blindfold, shutter, curtain, leading nowhere, screen, cover, shade, disguise, pretext, ruse, faint, subterfuge, pretence.

ant – conscious, seeing, aware, careful, open.

Bliss (noun)

syn – rapture, ecstasy, happiness, joy.

ant – misery, unhappiness.

Blithe (adjective)

syn – pleasant, warm, convivial, ebullient, elated, genial, jovial, light - hearted, cheerful, high-spirited, mirthful, joyous, gay.

ant – dismal, gloomy, melancholic.

Block (verb/ noun)

syn – obstruct, mould, shape, form, stiffen, brace, mass, thick piece, simpleton, close, bar, check, choke, jam, mould, impede, arrest, hinder.

ant – facilitate, open, ease, clear.

Blockhead (adjective)

syn – stupid, foolish, chump, dill, dolt, dunce, fool, idiot, ninny, nincompoop.

ant – humane, intelligent, wise.

Bloom (noun/verb)

syn – blossom, blush, flower, prime, burgeon, flourish, thrive, prosper.

ant – wilt, decay, die.

Blow (noun/ verb)

syn – stroke, knock, bang, box, cuff, punch, rap, slap, buffet, impact, calamity, disaster, misfortune, gale, blast, gust, pant, puff, gasp, drive, impel, sound, wind, beat, fight.

ant – caress, good fortune.

Blues (noun)

syn – depression, dejection, despondency, melancholy, sadness, doldrums, gloom.

ant – cheer, gaiety, merriment.

Blunder (noun/verb)

syn – fumble, bungle, blooper, boggle, botch,

muddle, mishandle, flounder, limp, shuffle, stagger.

Blunt (verb/adjective)

syn – dull, obtuse, stolid, insensible, abrupt, bluff, downright, rough, harsh, ungracious, rude, benumb, paralyse, deaden, stupefy, callous, mitigate, soften.

ant – sharp.

Blur (verb)

syn – becloud, befog, cloud, dim, dull, fog, eclipse, gloom, mist, obscure, overcast, overshadow.

ant – clear.

Blush (verb)

syn – flush, redden, colour, embarrassed.

ant – blanch, pale, whiten .

Boast (verb/ noun)

syn – brag, crow, gloat, pride, strut, vaunt, conceited, flaunt.

ant – humble, modest.

Boil (verb/noun)

syn – fry, poach, braise, saute, simmer, steam, stew, dry-fry, pot-roast.

ant – cool .

Boisterous (adjective)

syn – noisy, loud, roaring, stormy, obstreperous, turbulent, clamorous.

ant – quiet, calm.

Bold (adjective)

syn – aggressive, forward, pushing, fearless, enterprising, energetic, opportunistic, reckless, daring, valiant, undaunted, intrepid, brave, courageous, adventurous, confident,insolent, impudent, self-reliant, impertinent, pushing, conspicuous, striking, prominent, abrupt, stout - hearted, bold - spirited, gallant, self-reliant .

ant – timid, faint.

Bolt (noun/verb)

syn – jump, start, startle, engorge, swill, gulp, guzzle, flash, hasten, hurry, scoot, whisk, zip, zoom, whirl.

Bombastic (adjective)

syn – purple, turgid, orotund, formal.

ant – brief, precise, simple, terse.

Bona fide (adjective)

syn – actual, authentic, genuine, good, original, real, true, undoubted, unquestionable.

ant – spurious.

Bond (noun/verb)

syn – convention, agreement, pact, covenant, fetter, knot, ligament, ligature, yoke, manacle, handcuff, adhere, cleave, cling, cohere.

ant – severance, dissociation.

Bony (adjective)

syn – emaciated, gaunt, skeletal, wasted, lanky, weak.

ant – fat, curvaceous, buxom.

Boom (noun, verb)

syn – bang, blast, roar, thunder, growl, grumble, roll, rumble, flourish, prosper, thrive.

ant – bust, downfall.

Bore (noun, verb)

syn – tire, weary, drip, jerk, tedium.

ant – excite, interest.

Boss (noun)

syn – chief, commander, head, leader, maestro, master, supervisor, employer, foreman, manager.

ant – employee, junior, subordinate, underling.

Bother (verb/noun)

syn – disturb, harass, pester, plague, trouble, worry, anger, enrage, upset.

ant – comfort, console, placate, solace.

Bottom (noun/adjective)

syn – base, basis, bed, foot, footing, foundation, ground, seat, substratum, underside, posterior, low, behind, rear, center, heart, lowest, nethermost.

ant – top, peak, uppermost.

Bounce (noun)

syn – bound, jump, leap, spring, rebound, dismissal, ejection, eviction, ouster, elasticity, resilience, spring, suppleness, buoyancy, animation, dash, lively, pertness, vim, vigour, vivacity, zip, ginger, pep, discharge, drop, release, terminate.

ant – dullness, apathy, listlessness.

Boundary (noun)

syn – border, bounds, confines, frontier, limit, edge, periphery, perimeter.

Bow (verb/noun)

syn – bend, incline, turn,

down, inflect, crook, curve, bend, prostrate, droop, depress, sink, crush, subdue, buckle, beak, stem, arc, crescent, curve, fore.

ant – resist, straighten.

Boycott (verb)

syn – shun, ostracise, blackball.

Brace (noun/verb)

syn – couple, duet, duo, match, pair, buttress, prop, fortify, gird, ready, steel, strengthen.

Brag (noun/verb/adjective)

syn – boast, crow, braggart, capital, excellent, prime, superb, superior.

Brainy (adjective)

syn – brilliant, intellectual, intelligent, knowing, knowledgeable.

ant – dimwitted, moron.

Brashness (adjective)

syn – brass, cheek, gall, hide, nerve, sauciness, conceit, effrontery, overbearing.

ant – civility, politeness, courtesy.

Brave (adjective/verb/noun)

syn – bold, courageous, dauntless, fearless, gallant, heroic, intrepid, plucky, undaunted, valiant, valorous, daring, reckless.

ant – coward, timid.

Brawl (verb/noun)

syn – quarrel, dispute, wrangle, bicker, squabble, altercation, scuffle, feud, tumultuous, row, outbreak, fray.

ant – peace, concurrence.

Breach (noun)

syn – rupture, opening, chasm, gap, fissure, rift, alienation, falling out, schism, difference, variance.

ant – observance, reconciliation.

Break (verb/noun)

syn – interlude, intermission, interval, lull, pause, recess, respite, spell, let-up, burst, crack, crush, fracture, shatter, shiver, smash, destroy, explode.

ant – mend, strengthen, make.

Breath (noun)

syn – exhalation, dash, hair, hint, intimation, shade, tinge, whiff, whisper, soul, spirit, vitality.

Breed (verb/noun)

syn – produce, upbringing, cause, kind, sort.

ant – sterile, fecund.

Breeze (noun/verb)

syn – zephyr, air, blast, blow, gust, wind, gale, cinch, walkover, child's play.

Brief (noun/verb)

syn – short, succinct, outline, barrister's guidelines for a case.

ant – lengthy, cumbersome.

Bright (adjective)

syn – beaming, brilliant, shining, radiant, resplendent, glowing, effulgent, incandescent, luminous, sparkling.

ant – dim, dull.

Brilliant (adjective/noun)

syn – bright, sparkling, distinguished, admirable, clever.

ant – dull, lackluster.

Brim (noun)

syn – edge, shore, border, bank, margin, coast, skirt, vlrge, rim, brink.

ant – centre.

Brink (noun)

syn – border, brim, borderline, rim, verge, margin, fringe, edging, point, threshold, periphery.

ant – epicenter, nucleus.

Bristle (verb)

syn – anger, seethe, fume, rage, blow up, burn, explode, flare up, foam, abound, flow, swarm, teem.

Broad (adjective)

syn – ample, spacious, wide, expansive, liberal, comprehensive, extended, sweeping, large, widespread, clear, plain, unmistakable, unsubtle.

ant – narrow.

Broil (noun/verb)

syn – bake, burn, roast, swelter, quarrel, noisy fight, row, tumult, brawl, caterwaul, wrangle.

Broken-Hearted (adjective)

syn – disconsolate, comfortless, cheerless, inconsolable, sorrowful, melancholy, forlorn, undone, hopeless, despairing, woebegone, crushed.

ant – delighted, happy, joyous.

Brook (verb/noun)

syn – abide, accept, bear, endure, go, sustain, swallow, take, tolerate, withstand, stream, creek, branch.

Browbeat (verb)

syn – bludgeon, bully, cow, hector, intimidate, menace, threaten, bulldoze.

Brusque (adjective)

syn – abrupt, bluff, blunt, curt, gruff, short, surly, unceremonious, discourteous, ungracious, impolite, rude, terse.

ant – diplomatic, polite, gracious.

Bug (noun/verb)

syn – wog, spider, insect, arachnid, arthropod, beetle, crustacean, virus, irritate, annoy, vex, install a microphone.

ant – please.

Build (verb)

syn – erect, construct, fabricate, make, create, establish, develop, base, form,.

ant – break, destroy.

Buoyant (adjective)

syn – floating, light, cheerful, lively, resilient, blithe, animated, gay, jocund, spirited, elated, jubiliant.

ant – heavy, despondent.

Burly (adjective)

syn – huge, stout, bulky, strong, portly.

ant – frail.

Burn (verb/noun)

syn – scald, char, singe, brand, heat, cauterize, scorch, sear, feel strongly for, alight, hot.

ant – extinguish.

Bustle (verb/noun)

syn – hurry, fuss, fidget, flurry, tumult, ado, commotion, hustle.

ant – calm, tranquil, serenity.

Busy (adjective)

syn – active, engaged, engrossed, occupied, diligent.

ant – free, idle.

Buxom (Adjective)

syn – health, well-fed, plump, rounded, curvy, hearty.

ant – bony, emaciated. –

C

Cabal (noun)

syn – collusion, conspiracy, connivance, intrigue, plot, machination, scheme.

Cabinet (noun)

syn – shelves, drawers, cupboard, parliament.

Cache (noun/verb)

syn – inventory, reserve, reservoir, stock, store, bury, plant, stash, conceal.

Cackle (verb/noun)

syn – laugh, giggle, titter, babble, prattle, snicker.

ant – groan, cry.

Cacophonous (adjective)

syn – discordant, dissonant, rude, inharmonious, out of tune.

ant – musical, melodious.

Cadence (noun)

syn – beat, measure, meter, rhythm, swing.

Cadge (verb)

syn – beg, request, ask as charity, bum.

Cagey (adjective)

syn – astute, canny, knowing, shrewd, slick, smart, wise, perspicacious.

Cajole (verb)

syn – coax, persuade, beguile, wheedle, entrap, inveigle.

Calamity (noun)

syn – misfortune, disaster, catastrophe, mishap, trouble, hardship, mischance, affliction, adversity.

ant – blessing.

Calculating (adjective)

syn – crafty, scheming, designing, manipulative .

ant – straightforward, genuine.

Call (noun/verb)

syn – allure, appeal, charisma, charm, draw, fascination, glamour, lure, magnetism, necessity, reason, shout, yell, holler, whoop, visit, assemble, cluster, collect, congregate, convene, gather, group, come over, drop by, muster, characterize, label, tag, term, telephone, communicate, buzz, ring.

Calling (noun)

syn – art, business, career, craft, employment, job, line, occupation, profession, pursuit, trade, vocation, work, mission.

Callous (adjective)

syn – thick-skinned, insensitive, unfeeling, dull, obtuse, apathetic, indifferent.

ant – tender, sensitive.

Calm (adjective/verb/ noun)

syn – placid, quiet, unruffled, serene, peaceful, smooth, tranquil, still, impassive, composed, self - possessed, collected, repose, hush, soothe, appease, assuage, mollify.

ant – turbulent, stormy, agitated.

Calumny (noun)

syn – aspersion, defamation, denigration, slander, vilification, detraction, scandal.

ant – praise, flattery.

Campaign (noun)

syn – crusade, drive, movement, push, action.

Cancel (verb)

syn – abolish, abrogate, annihilate, annul, invalidate, negate, nullify, vitiate, void, delete, efface, erase, neutralize, expunge, obliterate, wipe out.

ant – continue, extend.

Candid (adjective)

syn – frank, honest, bluff, ingenuous, truthful, straightforward, plain, guileless.

ant – sly, wily, devious.

Cannonade (noun/ verb)

syn – barrage, bombardment, burst, salvo, shower, pepper, fusillade, storm, volley.

ant – peace, quiet.

Cantankerous (adjective)

syn – crabbed, cranky, ill-tempered, disagreeable, fretful, grumpy, testy, surly, peevish, petulant, irritable, nasty, snappy, irascible, grouchy.

ant – agreeable, pleasant, pleasing.

Capability (noun)

syn – ability, capacity, faculty, competence.

ant – incapability.

Caper (noun, verb)

syn – antic, frolic, joke, lark, prank, cavort, dance, frisk, gambol, romp.

Capitulate (verb)

syn – bow, buckle, submit, surrender, yield, succumb.

ant – resist.

Caprice (noun)

syn – conceit, fancy, freak, humor, impulse, notion, vagary, whim.

Captain (noun, verb)

syn – commander, leader, command, lead, precede.

ant – team player, follower.

Captivate (verb)

syn – charm, enchant, fascinate, enamour, catch, bewitch.

ant – release, free, liberate.

Capture (verb)

syn – gain, get, take, win, catch, net, secure.

ant – release, liberate.

Cardinal (adjective)

syn – capital, chief, major, main, first, foremost, key, leading, primary, principal, top, paramount.

ant – secondary, optional.

Care (noun/verb)

syn – mind, minister, tend, angst, anxiety, concern, disquietude, distress, solicitude, unease, trouble, worry, caution, heed, regard, mindfulness, charge, custody, keeping, trust, precaution, fastidiousness, painstaking, thoroughness, scrupulousness, regimen, therapy, treatment.

ant – neglect, disregard, ignore.

Careful (adjective)

syn – anxious, concerned, troubled, uneasy, heedful, mindful, thoughtful, cautious, circumspect, vigilant, discreet, wary, conscientious, meticulous, punctilious, scrupulous.

ant – careless, remiss, negligent.

Caress (verb/noun)

syn – cuddle, dandle, hug, neck, fondle, pet, smooch, show affection.

ant – blow, punish.

Caretaker (noun)

syn – custodian, guardian, keeper, conservator.

Caricature (verb/noun)

syn – burlesque, send - up, take -off, travesty, mimicry, parody.

Carnage (noun)

syn – bloodshed, violence, massacre, slaughter, butchery, havoc.

ant – peace, tranquility.

Carnal (adjective)

syn – animal, fleshy, physical, sensual, bodily.

ant – moral, spiritual.

Carry (verb)

syn – bear, bring, convey, haul, take, transport, hold, transmit, accept, adopt, transfer, win, affected, conduct, behave, move, practise, postpone, complete .

ant – leave, drop.

Carousal (noun)

syn – binge, drinking bout, spree, brannigan.

ant – restraint, abstinence.

Cartel (noun)

syn – alliance, bloc, coalition, confederacy, federation, league, union, organization, pool, syndicate, trust.

Carve (verb)

syn – cleave, cut, sever, slice, slit, split, engrave, etch, incise.

Case (noun/ verb)

syn – instant, event, example, matter, problem, patient, agreement, lawsuit , circumstances, container, box, covering.

Cast (noun/verb)

syn – bent, bias, disposition, leaning, penchant, predilection, proclivity, propensity, tendency, trend, aspect, countenance, expression, visage, form, pattern, shape, breed, description, ilk, kind, manner, nature, order, stamp, type, variety, fling, heave, hurl, launch, pitch, sling, throw, hue, tinge, tint, total, sum up, aim, direct, head, level, train, turn, calculate, compute, chart, contrive, design, frame, plan, work out, emit, radiate, shed, throw, project, hunt, look, quest, search, seek, banish, dismiss, dispel, shut out.

ant – keep, retain.

Castigate (verb)

syn – criticize, admonish, chastise, chide, dress down, rebuke, reproach, reprimand, scold, upbraid, correct, lambaste, discipline.

ant – reward, praise.

Casual (adjective)

syn – accidental, chance, contingent, inadvertent, informal, easy, natural, relaxed, spontaneous.

ant – formal, stiff, planned.

Catastrophe (noun)

syn – misfortune, calamity, disaster, mishap, debacle, cataclysm, mischance.

ant – blessing, boon, fortune.

Catch (verb/noun)

syn – seize, grasp, snatch, clutch, gripe, grapple, snare, trap, charm, captivate, surprise, overtake, arrest, apprehend, enmesh, capture.

ant – drop, release.

Category (noun)

syn – class, order, set, classification, group.

Cause(noun/verb)

syn – ground, motive, motivation, reason, start, antecedent, call, ground, justification, necessity, action, case, instance, bring about, effect, effectuate, generate, induce, lead to, secure, trigger.

ant – effect, consequence.

Cautious (adjective)

syn – careful, wary, discreet, circumspect, guarded, prudent, heedful.

ant – reckless, imprudent.

Cave (noun/verb)

syn – burrow, cavern , grotto, tunnel, fall in, collapse.

Cavil (verb)

syn – carp, niggle, pettifog, quibble.

ant – support, endorse.

Cavort (verb)

syn – caper, dance, frisk, frolic, gambol, rollick, romp.

Cease (noun/verb)

syn – stop, stay, desist, terminate, discontinue, quit, end.

ant – begin, start.

Cede (verb)

syn – abandon, abdicate, demit, forswear, hand over, relinquish, forgo, resign, surrender, waive, deed, grant, alienate, assign, convey, transfer.

ant – keep, retain.

Celebration (noun)

syn – ball, banquet, feast, festival, party, rite, festivity, praise.

ant – funeral, mourning.

Celerity (noun)

syn – dispatch, expedition, fleetness, haste, hurry, hustle, rapidity, speed, swiftness.

ant – slowness, leisure.

Celestial (adjective)

syn – divine, heavenly, paradise, empyreal.

ant – earthly.

Censorious (adjective)

syn – captious, carping, critical, fault finding.

ant – flattering, complimentary.

Censure (noun)

syn – disapproval, reproach, disapprobation, rebuke, reprimand, stricture, chide, reprehend.

ant – approval, praise.

Centre (noun/verb)

syn – core, heart, hub, middle, midst, kernel, main object, principal place.

ant – boundary, edge, perimeter.

Ceremonious (adjective)

syn – conventional, courtly, formal, ritual, courtly.

ant – informal, casual.

Certain (adjective)

syn – sure, specific, undefined, limited, assumed.

ant – uncertain, doubtful, unlikely.

Chafe (verb)

syn – irritate, be impatient, vex, annoy, bug.

ant – soothe.

Chagrin (noun/verb)

syn – vexation, annoyance, humiliation, displeasure, ill - humour, provoke, disquiet, mortify.

ant – pleasure.

Chain (noun/verb)

syn – bind, lock, fasten, shackle, series.

ant – loosen, release.

Challenge (noun/verb)

syn – contest, doubt, objection, call to contest, take exception to, defiance, exception.

ant – pass.

Champion (verb/adjective)

syn – advocate, recommend, back, endorse, uphold, support, ace, prime, quality, splendid, superior, terrific.

ant – loser, mediocre.

Chance (noun/verb)

syn – accidental, contingent, fortuity, fortune, risk, peril, hazard, gamble, opportunity, adventitious, incidental, provisional, random, happen, befall, occur, take place.

ant – inevitable, inexorable.

Change (verb/noun)

syn – exchange, substitute, alter, modify, convert, transfigure, transform, transmute, transmogrify, addition, build, devise.

ant – stabilise, sustain.

Chaos (noun)

syn – confusion, disorder, disarray, anarchy, haywire, upside down.

ant – order.

Characteristic (adjective/noun)

syn – attribute, feature, mark, peculiarity, trait, quality.

ant – general.

Charade (noun)

syn – make believe, pretense.

ant – genuine, sincere, honest.

Charisma (noun)

syn – allure, appeal, call, charm, enticement, lure, magnetism, witchery, draw.

ant – repulsive, ugliness.

Charge (verb/noun)

syn – accuse, payment, debt, attack, command, instruct, fill, supply, care, responsibility, command, load, burden, ascribe, impute, arraign, impeach, indict, tax, order, bid, enjoin, custody, trust, cost, expense, price, sum, charged, onslaught, encounter.

ant – clear, retreat, relieve.

Charming (adjective)

syn – pleasing, bewitching, captivating, winning, enchanting, elegant, entrancing, fascinating, lively, alluring, delightful.

ant – ugly, repulsive.

Chart (noun/verb)

syn – table, tabulation, blueprint, contrive, design, devise, frame, plan, project, scheme, strategize, work out.

Chary (adjective)

syn – canny, economical, frugal, provident, careful, cautious, circumspect, forehanded, prudent, wary.

ant – extravagant, heedless.

Chase (verb)

syn – pursue, follow, hunt, drove, engraving.

ant – lead, precede.

Chastise (verb)

syn – admonish, castigate, chide, dress down, rebuke, reprimand, reprove, scold, upbraid, correct, discipline.

ant – reward, praise, commend.

Chasm (noun)

syn – gorge, cleft, difference, gap, opening, fissure, cavity.

Chaste (adjective)

syn – continent, pure, virtuous, modest, innocent, uncorrupt, refined.

ant – corrupt.

Chastity (noun)

syn – modesty, decency, innocence, purity, virtue, virginity.

ant – promiscuity.

Chattel (noun)

syn – portable property, belonging, personal effects, possession.

Chatter (verb/noun)

syn – babble, gibber, jabber, prate, prattle, yak.

ant – quiet, silence, reticence.

Chaw (verb)

syn – champ, chew, chomp, chump, crunch, masticate, munch.

Cheap (adjective)

syn – inexpensive, low cost, lousy, miserable, shoddy, sleazy, close-fisted, paltry.

ant – expensive, high-priced.

Cheat (verb/noun)

syn – con, defraud, fleece, swindle, victinise, deceive, rob, theft, trick, dupe, beguile, mislead, inveigle, swindle, embezzle, befool, dishonest, trickster, impostor, rogue, charlatan, mountebank, knave.

Check (verb/noun)

syn – stop, restrain, investigate, match, correspond, mark, hinder, control.

ant – advance, encourage.

Checkmate (verb)

syn – baffle, balk, check, defeat, foil, stump, frustrate, stymie, thwart.

Cheekiness (noun)

syn – assumption, audacity, boldness, cheek, brashness, insolence, effrontery, gall, pertness, sassiness, incivility, nerve.

ant – respect, reverence.

Cheer (verb/noun)

syn – encourage, applaud, gladden, warm, exhilarate, joy, liveliness, merriment.

ant – depress, gloom.

Cheerful (adjective)

syn – cheery, blithe, happy, sunny, winsome, sprightly, animated, gay, joyous, merry, mirthful, sunny, gleeful.

ant – gloomy, melancholy.

Cherish (verb)

syn – appreciate, esteem, prize, respect, treasure, value.

ant – ignore, neglect, disregard.

Cherubic (adjective)

syn – babyish, childlike, infantile.

ant – elderly, aged.

Chic (adjective)

syn – dashing, fashionable, mod, posh, smart, stylish, swanky, trig, trendy.

ant – dowdy, unkempt.

Chicanery (noun)

syn – craft, craftiness, deviousness, dishonesty, slyness, trickery, shiftiness.

ant – sincerity, genuineness.

Chief (noun/adjective)

syn – boss, leader, foreman, head, manager, overseer, chieftain, principal, master, cardinal, first, foremost, key, main, major, top.

ant – secondary, subordinate.

Chink (noun)

syn – break, cleavage, cleft, crack, crevice, fissure, rift, split.

Child (noun)

syn – baby, infant, toddler, youngster, offspring, innocent, immature, gullible.

ant – adult.

Childish (adjective)

syn – childlike, juvenile, immature, infantile, puerile, foolish, silly, young, trifling.

ant – mature.

Chill (noun/verb)

syn – depression, uneasiness, make cold, dampen, discourage, hostility, aloofness.

ant – warmth, heat.

Chimera (noun)

syn – illusion, dream, imagination, hope, fantasy, unreal, fanciful image.

ant – reality.

Chip (noun/verb)

syn – piece, slice, mark, dent, disc, counter, contribute, interrupt.

ant – whole, total.

Chisel (verb)

syn – bilk, cheat, cozen, defraud, gull, mulct, rook, swindle, victimise, trim.

Chivalry (noun)

syn – politeness, courtesy, virtue, honour, courage, duty.

ant – discourtesy.

Choke (noun/verb)

syn – cork, fill, plug, stopper, strangle, throttle, smother, stifle, suffocate, clog, close, cork, repress, squelch, quench, squash.

Choleric (adjective)

syn – angry, indignant, mad, testy, irascible, touchy.

Choose (verb)

syn – cull, elect, pick, select, prefer, pitch, decide, discriminate.

ant – reject.

Chore (noun)

syn – effort, task, assignment, duty, job, office, stint, work.

Chronic (adjective)

syn – habitual, routine, continuing, prolonged, protracted, inveterate, lingering, persistent.

ant – temporary, fleeting.

Chronicle (noun)

syn – annals, history, account, description, narration, statement, story, report.

Chuck (verb)

syn – discard, dispose, dump, junk, jettison, ditch, bump, dismiss, eject, evict, expel, oust.

ant – accept, embrace, keep.

Chump (noun/verb)

syn – clod, dolt, blockhead, dimwit, dunce, crunch, masticate, chew, chomp.

ant – genius, intellectual.

Churlish (adjective)

syn – bad- tempered, rustic, peasant, rude, impolite, brutish, sullen, crabby, snarling, stingy, miserly, mean.

ant – polite, generous.

Churn (verb)

syn – agitate, convulse, rock, shake, boil, bubble, burn, ferment, seethe, simmer.

ant – calm, soothe.

Chutzpah (noun)

syn – assumption, audacity, cheek, sauciness, pertness, effrontery, gall, impertinence, nerve, brazenness, disrespect.

ant – courtesy, regard.

Cinch (noun/verb)

syn – pushover, child's play, breeze, certainty, sure thing, assure, ensure, guarantee, secure, warrant.

Circle (noun/verb)

syn – round, group, range, ring.

Circuit (noun)

syn – beat, round, route, band, circle, ring, cycle, orbit, ambit, compass, periphery, association, league, loop, gyration, turn, wheel, whirl, revolution, rotation.

Circulate (verb)

syn – advertise, blazon, broadcast, disperse, disseminate, propagate, spread, distribute, diffuse, disperse, radiate, scatter, spread, strew.

ant – restrict.

Circumlocution (noun)

syn – euphemism, indirectness, periphrasis, talkative, verbosity.

ant – brevity, terseness, conciseness.

Circumspect (adjective)

syn – careful, cautious, chary, forehanded, gingerly, prudent, chary.

ant – reckless, imprudent.

Circumstances (noun)

syn – condition, situation, position, surroundings, environment, state.

Circumscribe (verb)

syn – bound, contain, encircle, enclose, envelope, surround, encompass, limited, defined.

Cite (verb)

syn – quote, refer, adduce, commend, summon, call.

City (noun)

syn – hamlet, suburb, town, village, metropolis, megalopolis.

ant – village.

Civic (adjective)

syn – civil, national, public.

Civil (adjective)

syn – genteel, polite, courteous, well-bred, well-mannered, national, public.

Civilized (adjective)

syn – cultivated, cultured, educated, polished, refined, urbane, well-bred.

ant – uncivilized, barbaric.

Claim (verb/noun)

syn – title, right, say, demand, require, ask, assert, obtain a title.

ant – waive.

Clamor (noun/verb)

syn – babel, din, hubbub, noise, racket, tumult, uproar, pandemonium, bawl, bellow, roar, uproar, shout, whoop, yell.

ant – silence, tranquility, calm.

Clandestine (adjective)

syn – covert, secret, undercover, cloak-and-dagger, hush-hush.

ant – public, open.

Claptrap (noun)

syn – bombast, rant, turgidity, grandiloquence, nonsense, piffle, baloney, crap, blather, drivel, bilge.

ant – knowledge.

Clarify (verb)

syn – elucidate, explain, explicate, interpret, purify.

ant – complicate, confuse, obscure.

Clash (noun/verb)

syn – altercation, argument, bicker, contention, controversy, quarrel, squabble, tiff, hassle, tangle, brush, encounter, run-in, spat, skirmish, conflict, confrontation, difference, discord, faction, friction, schism, strife, war.

ant – harmony, concurrence.

Clasp (verb/ noun)

syn – grab, hook, catch, embrace, hug, grip, clutch, buckle, entwine.

ant – release, detach.

Class (verb/noun)

syn – caste, estate, order, elegance, sophistication, club, position, lesson.

Classic (adjective)

syn – archetypal, model, quintessential, vintage, prototypical, representative, classical.

ant – modern, contemporary.

Clean (adjective/adverb/verb)

syn – dust, polish, scour, scrub, sweep, tidy, wipe, orderly, cleanse, purify, unadulterated, spotless, stainfree, entire, whole, complete, pure, chaste, free from dirt, fresh, immaculate, sanitary.

ant – dirty, pollute, untidy.

Clear (verb/noun/adjective)

syn – definite, distinct, unmistakable, transparent, plain, open, free, certain, absolute, pay off, solve, clarify, tidy up, bright, unobstructed, lucid, visible, evident, obvious, musical, silvery, mellifluous, acquit, justify, exonerate, disengage, loosen, net, without deductions .

ant – vague, obscure.

Cleave (verb)

syn – carve, cut, dissever, slice, slit, split, adhere, bond, cling, cohere, stick, connect.

ant – assemble.

Clemency (noun)

syn – charity, grace, lenience, mercy, mercifulness.

ant – punishment, strictness.

Clergyman (noun)

syn – cleric, divine, minister, prelate, theologian, ecclesiastic.

ant – atheist.

Clever (adjective)

syn – quick, intelligent, skilful, able, ingenious, adroit, adept, quick – witted.

ant – stupid.

Click (noun/verb)

syn – clack, snap, connect, relate, come off, go, succeed, work out.

ant – clash, fail.

Climax (noun/verb)

syn – acme, apex, crest, crown, height, peak, summit, zenith, cap, crest, crown, culmination.

Climb (verb)

syn – ascent, mount, rise, scale, clamber, arise, surmount, come up.

ant – descend, fall.

Clique (noun)

syn – circle, coterie, group, set, party, gang, brotherhood.

Cloak (noun)

syn – long dress, cover, disguise, robe, secrecy.

ant – expose .

Clobber (verb)

syn – hit, strike, defeat, beat, lick, wipe out.

ant – caress.

Clog (noun/verb)

syn – block, obstruct, hamper, choke, impede, impediment, hindrance, check, obstacle.

ant – clear.

Club (noun/verb)

syn – federation, fraternity, league, lodge, order, union, association, clique, golf stick, hit, strike.

Clumsy (adjective)

syn – awkward, ponderous, bungling, gawky, inept,

blundering, ungainly, lumbering, unwieldly, gauche.

ant – adroit, dexterous, skilful.

Clutter (verb)

syn – untidy, chaos, confusion, disarray, disorder, disorganised, jumble.

ant – order, method, sequence.

Coarse (adjective)

syn – crude, vulgar, rough, harsh, thick, large, unrefined, inelegant, unsophisticated .

ant – refined, smooth.

Coerce (verb)

syn – compel, force, restrain, check, curb, drive, constrain.

ant – coax, cajole.

Cold (adjective/noun)

syn – chill, unfriendly, hostile, antagonistic, unconscious, faint, neglected, left out, cool, indifference, unsympathetic, inhuman, icy, frigid, frosty, chilled, aloof, distant.

ant – hot, warm.

Coincide (verb)

syn – agree, correspond, jibe, tally, fit, exactly, concur, harmonise.

ant – clash.

Colour (noun/verb)

syn – dye, paint, stain, tinge, tint, pigment, interest, brightness, blush, influenced by, complexion.

ant – pallor, blanch, colourless

Collision (noun)

syn – opposition, crash, shock, clash, conflict.

ant – accord.

Combustible (adjective)

syn – burnable, flammable, inflammable.

ant – incombustible, non – inflammable.

Come (verb)

syn – arrive, gain, reach, approach, move, occur, happen, acquire, be, resultant, charge, arise, derive.

ant – go, depart, leave.

Comfort (verb/noun)

syn – ease, leisure, relaxation, relief, repose, rest, retire, cosy, snug, restful, cheer.

ant – agitate.

Comic (adjective)

syn – funny, farcical, droll, ludicrous, burlesque.

ant – tragic.

Command (verb/noun)

syn – deserve, overlook, direction, directive, order, instruction, injunction.

ant – obey, entreaty.

Commend (verb/noun)

syn – regard, commit, entrust, yield, praise, extol, laud, eulogise, recommend .

ant – censure.

Company (noun)

syn – guests, friends, associates, crew, organization.

Compassion (noun)

syn – pity, tenderness, kindness, sympathy, commiseration, mercy, clemency.

ant – cruelty, torture

Compel (verb)

syn – coerce, force, oblige, necessitate, constrain, bend, subject .

ant – coax, cajole.

Compete (verb)

syn – contend, oppose, rival, vie, contest, strive, struggle.

ant – ally, co–operate.

Competent (adjective)

syn – able, capable, fit, good, efficient, qualified .

ant – incompetent, incapable.

Complain (verb)

syn – beef, whine, bewail, gripe, grouse, complain.

ant – applaud, praise.

Compliant (adjective)

syn – accommodating, agreeable, suggestible, willing, obliging, complaisant, adaptable, malleable, lenient.

ant – wilful, stubborn.

Complete (adjective/verb)

syn – finished, over, whole, perfect, effect, terminate, accomplish, execute, conclude, fulfill, realise, achieve, attain, consummate.

ant – incomplete, unfinished.

Complex (adjective)

syn – complicated, tangled, intricate, knotty, mixed, composite, manifold, mingled, obsession.

ant – simple, straightforward.

Compose (verb)

syn – make, form, constitute, settle, reconcile, control, make calm, quiet, tranquil, sedate, make music , write.

ant – disorganise, disturb.

Composition (noun)

syn – article, dissertation, essay, exercise, paper, theme, thesis, treatise, musical piece, report.

Compromise (noun/ verb)

syn – agreement, concession, settlement, adjustment, imperil, put at risk, jeopardise, commit.

ant – differ, protect.

Compulsory (adjective)

syn – necessary, binding, imperative, mandatory, obligatory, sure, requisite.

ant – optional.

Compunction (noun)

syn – regret, uneasiness, guilt, shame.

ant – satisfaction.

Conceited (adjective)

syn – boastful, proud, vain, vainglorious, egotistical, opinionated, confident, cocksure, overbearing .

ant – modest.

Concern (verb/noun)

syn – regard, interest, importance, involve, worry, unhappiness, anxiety, business, enterprise.

ant – unconcern, disregard.

Conclusive (adjective)

syn – final, decisive, definitive, determining, significant.

ant – tentative, provisional.

Condescend (verb)

syn – patronise, stoop, deign, tolerate, unbend.

ant – revere, respect.

Confidence (noun/verb)

syn – trust, aplomb, cockiness, poise, self-assurance, smugness, self-possession, secret, privately, jaunty, zest.

ant – anxiety, doubt, diffidence.

Confirm (verb)

syn – settle, agree upon, assure, fix, establish, ratify, verify, vouch, endorse, bind, corroborate.

ant – deny, refute.

Confine (verb)

syn – shut, gaol, imprison, intern, incarcerate, restrict, limit.

ant – release, liberate.

Confuse (verb)

syn – puzzle, bewilder, confound, nonplus, dumbfound, perplex, baffle, mystify, astonish, amaze, abash, flurry, discompose, make doubtful.

ant – clarify, enlighten.

Connect (verb)

syn – joint, cohere, combine, attach, couple, link, unite, interlock, hyphenate, involve, meet .

ant – sever, separate, dissociate.

Conquer (verb)

syn – defeat, vanquish, prevail upon, win, suceed, triumph, beat, quell, rout, subjugate, discomfit, overthrow, crush, humble, overpower.

ant – surrender, lose.

Consent (verb/noun)

syn – agree, assent, concur, subscribe, acquiesce, accept, permit, approval, endorse, submit .

ant – dissent, demur, contradict.

Conserve (verb/noun)

syn – hoard, maintain, preserve, save, store, keep, protect, sustain, uphold.

ant – disperse, scatter, squander.

Consider (verb)

syn – believe, think, deliberate, count, deem, reckon, regard, study, heed, ponder.

Considerate (adjective)

syn – attentive, diplomatic, helpful, tactful, thoughtful, caring, kind, humane, benevolent.

ant – inconsiderate, heedless.

Console (verb/noun)

syn – comfort, cheer, condole, solace, sympathize, soothe, relieve, bracket, closet, ancone.

ant – aggravate, grieve.

Constant (adjective)

syn – fixed, stable, unmoving, steadfast, firm, enduring, permanent, abiding, invariable, regular, resolute, uniform, unwavering, tenacious, unremitting, unswerving, incessant, continual, sustained.

ant – variable, fickle.

Consult (verb)

syn – confer, counsel, negotiate, parley, deliberate, advice.

ant – argue.

Contemplate (verb)

syn – think, ponder, consider, gaze, survey, meditate, reflect, muse.

ant – ignore.

Contemptible (adjective)

syn – despicable, detestable, execrable, depraved, reprehensible, repulsive.

ant – admirable.

Contemptuous (adjective)

syn – audacious, disdainful, insolent, scornful, supercilious, hostile, overbearing.

ant – considerate, reverent.

Contented (adjective)

syn – content, pleased, gratified, satisfied, at ease, appeased, comfortable.

ant – discontented.

Contradict (verb)

syn – deny, contravene, controvert, disprove, oppose, refute, gainsay.

ant – concur, agree.

Control (verb/noun)

syn – direct, govern, manage, regulate, rule, supervise, restrain, command, possess.

ant – free.

Controversy (noun)

syn – conflict, contention, debate, discord, dispute, dissension, friction, arguement, bickering, quarrel, strife, wrangle .

ant – consensus, agreement.

Conversation (noun)

syn – chat, dialogue, talk, discussion, colloquy, chatter.

ant – reticence.

Convulsion (noun)

syn – fit, spasm, seizure, paroxysm, contortion .

Copy (noun/verb)

syn – duplicate, facsimile, model, replica, specimen, reproduction, imitate, counterpart.

ant – original, prototype.

Cordial (adjective)

syn – warm, pleasant, affectionate, hearty, ardent, liquor.

ant – distant, aloof.

Corpse (noun)

syn – body , stiff, remains, cadaver.

Corrupt (verb/adjective)

syn – contaminate, defile, pollute, infect, spoil, pervert, vitiate, falsify, bribe, rotten, tainted, wicked, dishonest, putrid.

ant – virtuous, purify, edify.

Counterpart (noun)

syn – complement, correlate, opposite, number, parallel, similar.

ant – antithesis, contrast.

Countless (adjective)

syn – infinite, immeasurable, incalculable, innumerable .

ant – numbered, calculable.

Courage (noun)

syn – bravery, grit, guts, nerve, pluck, resolution, fortitude, effrontery.

ant – cowardice.

Covenant (noun)

syn – agreement, compact, contract, concordat.

Crack (verb/noun)

syn – breach, chink, cleft, crevice, fissure, hole, solve, open, attempt, first light of dawn.

ant – mend, resist.

Crazy (adjective)

syn – mad, fanatic, deranged, demented, distracted, insane.

ant – sane, sensible.

Create (verb)

syn – compose, design, make, produce, invent, build, mould, devise.

ant – destroy, obliterate.

Creed (noun)

syn – doctrine, tenet, dogma, idea, opinion.

Crime (noun)

syn – felony, offence, treason, violation, misdemeanour,

ant – benefaction, service.

Crone (noun)

syn – beldam, hag, witch, ugly, frightening woman.

ant – beautiful, charming.

Crony (noun)

syn – associate, comrade, chum, fellow, mate, buddy,

pal, companion.

ant – adversary, opponent.

Crook (noun/verb)

syn – bend, bow, curve, turn, bilk, cheat, rook, trickster, swindler, angle, arch.

ant – straight, honest.

Cross (noun/verb/adjective)

syn – affliction, burden, trial, tribulation, annul, cancel, erase, expunge, obliterate, intersect, baffle, checkmate, defeat, thwart, stymie, demolish, destroy, ruin, shatter, wreck, pass, track, transit, bad-tempered, grumpy, grouchy, irritable, irascible, testy, surly, petulant, disagreeable.

Crouch (verb)

syn – huddle, hunch, squat, hunker.

Crown (noun/verb)

syn – acme, apex, climax, crest, height, peak, pinnacle, summit, top, roof, vertex, cap, top off.

Crucial (adjective)

syn – acute, urgent, pressing, critical .

ant – trivial.

Crucify (verb)

syn – rack, torment, torture, pain.

Cruel (adjective)

syn – ferocious, fierce, savage, vicious, truculent, wolfish, bestial, inhuman, feral.

ant – kind, merciful, humane.

Crumble (verb)

syn – break down, dissolve, decompose, disintegrate, fragment.

ant – construct, assemble, build.

Crumple (noun/verb)

syn – crease, crimp, crinkle, fold, pleat, pucker, buckle, cave in, collapse, give, go.

ant – smooth.

Crunch (verb)

syn – champ, chew, masticate, munch, gnash, grind.

Crusade (noun)

syn – cause, campaign, drive, movement, push, action.

Crush (noun/verb)

syn – mass, mob, multitude, swarm, throng, infatuation, break, destroy, ruin, mash, pulp, squash, granulate, grind, mill, engulf, overcome, overpower, annihilate, drub, smash, vanquish, express, press, squeeze.

ant – win, conquer.

Crust (noun)

syn – assumption, audacity, boldness, nerve, insolence, effrontery, sauce, cheek, disrespect, gall, impudence, pertness, brazenness, impertinence, chutzpah.

ant – courtesy, regard.

Crutch (noun)

syn – brace, buttress, prop, shore, support.

Cry (verb/noun)

syn – bellow, yell, shriek, shout, scream, roar, outcry, screech, howl, bawl, lament.

ant – laugh.

Cryptic (adjective)

syn – arcane, cabalistic, enigmatic, mysterious, mystic, occult, puzzling.

Crystalline (adjective)

syn – clear, limpid, lucid, pellucid, transparent, see-through.

ant – obscure, vague.

Cuddle (verb)

syn – nestle, snug, snuggle, caress, fondle, pat, pet, nuzzle.

Cue (noun)

syn – clue, hint, intimation, suggestion.

Cul-de-sac (noun)

syn – blind alley, dead end.

Culpable (adjective)

syn – guilty, blameworthy, reprehensible, censurable.

ant – innocent, praiseworthy.

Cultured (adjective)

syn – civilized, polished, elegant, refined, urbane, educated, well-bred.

ant – coarse, boorish, uncouth.

Cumbersome (adjective)

syn – heavy, lumpy, ponderous.

ant – light, easy.

Cumulate (verb)

syn – aggregate, garner, gather, agglomerate, amass, accrue, accumulate, collect, hive.

ant – disperse, distribute, discard.

Cunning (noun/adjective)

syn – art, artfulness, artifice,

craft, guile, slyness, duplicity, shape, wily, foxy, deception, scheming.

ant – simple, honest.

Cupidity (noun)

syn – acquisitiveness, avarice, covetousness, greed.

ant – saturation, satisfaction, contentment.

Curb (noun/verb)

syn – check, control, constraint, cramp, limit, stricture, brake, bridle, inhibit, restrain, trammel.

ant – encourage.

Cure (noun/verb)

syn – physic, curative, remedy, nostrum, medicine, heal, corrective.

ant – illness, malady.

Curious (adjective)

syn – inquiring, investigative, questioning, nosy, snoopy, bizarre, cranky, eccentric, odd, peculiar, quaint, strange, weird, perplexing, queer.

ant – usual, routine.

Curl (verb)

syn – curve, wave, entwine, undulate, coil, corkscrew, meander, twist, weave, spiral.

ant – straighten.

Curse (noun/verb)

syn – affliction, bane, evil, scourge, anathema, jinx, blasphemy, oath, swear, expletive, rack, torment, torture, malediction.

ant – blessing, boon.

Cursory (adjective)

syn – hasty, superficial, scant, careless .

ant – thorough, careful, detailed .

Curt (adjective)

syn – abrupt, blunt, brief, brusque, crusty, gruff, short.

ant – loquacious, talkative.

Curtail (verb)

syn – abbreviate, abridge, condense, reduce, shorten.

ant – permit, increase.

Curve (noun/verb)

syn – crook, bend, bow, angle, arc, arch, wave, curl, undulate.

ant – straight.

Custody (noun)

syn – care, charge, guardianship, keeping, supervision, trust, charge, confinement, detention, ward.

ant – release, liberate.

Custom (noun/adjective)

syn – habit, manner, practice, use, way, customized, made-to-order, patronage, trade, traffic, rite, ritual.

Cut (verb/noun)

syn – gash, slash, slit, incision, penetrate, reduce, shorten.

ant – join, extend.

Cycle (noun)

syn – circle, circuit, orbit, tour, turn, round.

Cynic (noun/adjective)

syn – ironic, sardonic, wry, misanthropist.

D

Dab (noun/verb)

syn – bit, crumb, dash, drop, fragment, grain, iota, tittle, shred, trifle, whit, daub, plaster, smear, smirch.

Daft (adjective)

syn – crazy, demented, disordered, insane, mad, wrong, touched, distraught, nutty.

ant – sane, intelligent.

Daily (adjective/noun)

syn – everyday, quotidian, diurnal.

ant – nightly, nocturnal.

Damage (noun, verb)

syn – injury, harm, disable, hurt, weaken, wound, incapacitate.

ant – repair, treat.

Dainty (noun/adjective)

syn – delicacy, morsel, treat, choice, fussy, nice, choosy, elegant, particular, meticulous.

ant – coarse, rough.

Danger (noun)

syn – hazard, menace, jeopardy, risk, threat, peril .

ant – safety, security.

Daring (noun)

syn – adventurous, venturesome, bold, reckless.

ant – cautious, cowardly.

Dark (adjective/noun)

syn – not light, secret, angry, gloomy, dreary, grey, murky, sombre.

ant – bright, light.

Dart (verb)

syn – float, fly, sail, skim, bolt, bustle, flash, hurry, hasten, race, rocket, hurl, hurtle, pitch, sling, throw, toss.

Dash (verb/noun/interjection)

syn – throw, strike violently, rush, ruin frustrate, vigour, small quantity, drive, zest, energy, gusto, pep, verve, zing zip.

ant – listlessness, lethargy.

Date (noun/verb)

syn – appointment, assignation, engagement, rendezvous, tryst, go out.

Dawdle (verb)

syn – fiddle, trifle, fidget, idle.

ant – hurry, rush.

Day (noun)

syn – age, epoch, era, period, time, duration, existence, life, lifetime, span, term.

ant – night.

Daze (noun/verb)

syn – bewilderment, stupor, trance, fog, muddle, mystification, perplexity, stupefaction, stun.

ant – consciousness, awareness.

Dead (adjective/noun/adverb)

syn – deceased, departed, defunct, extinct, lifeless, complete, absolute, accurate, exhausted, abruptly.

ant – alive, existent.

Dearth (noun)

syn – absence, lack, want.

ant – excess, surplus.

Debacle (noun)

syn – breakdown, collapse, crash, smash, wreck.

Debate (noun/verb)

syn – discuss, contest, consider, deliberate, argue, dispute, reason, conflict, contention, dissension.

ant – agreement, concurrence.

Debar (verb)

syn – bar, count out, eliminate, except, exclude, keep out, disallow, enjoin, forbid, inhibit, outlaw, prohibit, proscribe, taboo.

ant – allow, permit.

Debase (verb)

syn – doctor, load, adulterate, stain, canker, degrade, demean, downgrade, vitiate, warp, brutalize, pervert, bestialize.

ant- commend, applaud.

Debauch(verb)

syn – lure, persuade, seduce, warp.

ant – chaste, purity.

Debonair (adjective)

syn – vivacious, sprightly, cheery, light – hearted, gracious, polite, buoyant, sophisticated, affable, refined.

ant – uncouth, melancholic.

Debt (noun)

syn – arrears, liability, obligation, due, indebtedness.

ant – repay, loan.

Decay (noun/verb)

syn – decomposition, disintegration, rot, spoilage, putrefaction, molder, taint.

ant – bloom, flourish, thrive.

Deception (noun)

syn – trick , artifice, deceit, chicanery, fraud, equivocation, cheating, guile, dupe.

ant – sincerity, candour

Decide (verb)

syn – determine, resolve, settle, consider, judge, choose,

ant – hesitate.

Declare (verb)

syn – announce, assert, pronounce, publish, aver, proclaim, affirm, asseverate.

ant – conceal, censor .

Decrease (verb/noun)

syn – abate, decline, drop, dwindle, fall, sink, subside, reduce, weaken, wane.

ant – increase, grow, escalate.

Dedicate (verb)

syn – devote, consecrate, hallow, award, entrust, respect.

ant – desecrate, dishonour.

Deduce (verb)

syn – conclude, deduct, draw, gather, infer, judge, understand.

Deem (verb)

syn – think, view, suppose, opine, consider, regard, judge, believe.

Defeat (verb/noun)

syn – beat, overpower, overthrow, drub, lick, wipe, frustrate, thwart, subjugate, vanquish.

ant – win, victory.

Defect (noun/verb)

syn – blemish, bug, fault, flaw, imperfection, shortcoming, deficiency, deficit, lack, paucity, abandon, desert, renegade.

ant – virtue, strength.

Deficit (noun)

syn – paucity, scantiness, scarcity, poverty, shortfall, lack, insufficiency.

ant – excess, surplus.

Deficient (adjective)

syn – inadequate, poor, unsatisfactory, wanting, scant, insufficient, incomplete, weak.

ant – abundant, surplus.

Definite (adjective)

syn – sure, certain, categorical, explicit, express, specific, unconditional, unequivocal, unqualified, absolute, overt, candid, clear.

ant – indefinite, tentative.

Deft (adjective)

syn – adroit, artful, dexterous, facile, handy, nimble, slick, skillful, clever.

ant – clumsy, shoddy.

Defy (verb)

syn – challenge, dare, brave, face, front, break, disobey, flout, transgress, violate.

ant – obey, follow.

Deject (verb)

syn – depress, dispirit, oppress, sadden, weigh down.

ant – happy, cheerful.

Delay (verb)

syn – detain, hold, keep, retard, postpone.

ant – quicken, speed.

Deliver (verb)

syn – birth, bear, bring forth, deal, give, administer, furnish, rescue, save, supply, transfer.

Deluge (noun/verb)

syn – cataclysm, cataract, downpour, flood, overflow, torrent, overwhelm, submerge, drown, flush.

ant – scarcity, absence.

Delusion (noun)

syn – false belief, fantasy, illusion, mirage, imagination, misleading opinion.

ant – reality, fact.

Demand (verb/noun)

syn – ask, claim, exact, order, request, require .

ant – relinquish, supply.

Demean (verb)

syn – cheapen, debase, degrade, downgrade, humble, humiliate, mortify.

ant – respect, regard.

Demolish (verb)

syn – destroy, raze, level, ruin, break, pulverise, dash.

ant – construct, build.

Demonstrate (verb)

syn – authenticate, bear out, confirm, corroborate, endorse, establish, evidence, prove, show, evince, exhibit, display, manifest, reveal, proclaim.

ant – hide, conceal.

Demur (verb)

syn – disagree, balk, boggle, recoil, shirk, shy, shrink .

ant – accede, consent.

Denial (noun)

syn – contradiction, disclaimer, negation, rejection, refusal, turn down.

ant – acceptance.

Dense (adjective)

syn – blockhead, dumb, obtuse, stupid, heavy, lush, luxuriant, rank, thick, close, compact, crowded, packed, thick, tight.

ant – sparse, light.

Deny (verb)

syn – contradict, contravene, controvert, disaffirm, negate, disallow, refuse, disavow, disown, reject, renounce, repudiate.

ant – accept, affirm.

Depreciate (verb)

syn – diminish, lessen, underrate, disparage, malign, decry, degrade, decline, fall.

ant – appreciate.

Depress (verb)

syn – cheapen, depreciate, devaluate, downgrade, lower, reduce, deject, dispirit, oppress, sadden, weigh down, drop.

ant – cheerful, rise, ascend.

Deprive (verb)

syn – dispossess, divest, rob, strip.

ant – give, provide.

Depraved (adjective)

syn – malicious, malevolent, corrupt, evil, vile, degenerate, heinous, infamous, nefarious, villainous, wicked, profligate, pervert .

ant – chaste, moral, pious.

Derange (verb)

syn – craze, madden, unbalance, unhinge, disarrange, disarray, disrupt, disturb, jumble, mess, mix up, muddle, tumble, unsettle, upset, disorder.

Derelict (adjective)

syn – abandoned, bereft, deserted, desolate, forlorn, forsaken, neglectful, negligent, lax, remiss.

ant – prosperous, luxuriant, thriving.

Deride (verb)

syn – gibe, jeer, jest, laugh, mock, ridicule, scoff, scout, twit.

ant – respect, regard.

Derogate (verb)

syn – deprecate, belittle, disparage, minimize, run down, denigrate, detract.

ant – praise, flatter, commend.

Descend (verb)

syn – lower, fall, sink, drop, decline.

ant – ascend, rise.

Describe (verb)

syn – narrate, recite, recount, rehearse, relate, report, tell, delineate, picture, portray, render, represent, depict.

Descry (verb)

syn – catch, detect, discern, espy, glimpse, spot, spy, distinguish, mark, mind, note, notice, observe, pick out.

ant – ignore, overlook.

Deserve (verb)

syn – earn, gain, get, merit, win.

Designate (verb)

syn – appoint, make, name, nominate, allocate, appropriate, assign, earmark, call, characterize, label, baptize, dub, entitle, term.

Design (verb)

syn – concoct, brew, scheme, plan, devise, project, invent, intend, purpose, draw, sketch, describe.

Despair (noun/verb)

syn – hopelessness, dejection, desperation, despondency, discouragement.

ant – hope.

Desperate (adjective)

syn – acute, critical, crucial, dire, despondent, forlorn, fierce, furious, intense, terrible, vehement, violent.

Despicable (adjective)

syn – abhorrent, abominable, antipathetic, contemptible, detestable, disgusting, filthy, foul, infamous, lousy, nasty, nefarious, odious, repugnant, rotten.

ant – admirable, adorable.

Despise (verb)

syn – scorn, contempt, spurn, disdain, hate, slight, disregard, abhor, loathe.

ant – admire, idolise.

Despondent (adjective)

syn – despairing, desperate, forlorn, hopeless.

ant – cheerful, hopeful.

Despotic (adjective)

syn – dictatorial, autocratic, tyrannical, oppressive, wilful, cruel, overbearing, authoritarian .

ant – democratic.

Destroy (verb)

syn – annihilate, demolish, raze, ruin, wreck, eradicate, exterminate, extinguish, uproot.

ant – create, build.

Devise (verb)

syn – conceive, invent, formulate, contrive, bequeath.

Dexterous (adjective)

syn – adroit, clever, skilful, handy, deft, expert, nimble–fingered.

ant – clumsy.

Difficult (adjective)

syn – tough, hard, exacting, arduous, obscure, perplexing, intricate, austere, rigid, hard to please.

ant – easy, simple.

Diligent (adjective)

syn – assiduous, industrious, persevering, sedulous, busy, careful, earnest, conscientious.

ant – lazy, slothful.

Dirty (adjective)

syn – filthy, foul, soiled, sordid, unclean, squalid, lewd, repulsive, vulgar.

ant – clean, pure.

Disagree (verb)

syn – bicker, cavil, differ,

dissent, object, quibble, contradict, demur, upset.

ant – agree, concur.

Disapproval (noun)

syn – aspersion, blame, criticism, reprehension, rebuke.

ant – approval, praise.

Discerning (adjective)

syn – discriminating, astute, sharp, piercing, acute, clear – sighted, hawk–eyed , perspicacious.

ant – obtuse.

Discipline (noun/verb)

syn – order, rules, branch of learning , castigate, chasten, chastise, correct.

ant – indiscipline, indulgence.

Disclose (verb)

syn – uncover, expose, reveal, betray, tell, divulge, exhibit, unveil, bare.

ant – suppress, conceal.

Discourage (verb)

syn – deter, divert, dissuade, quell, subdue .

ant – encourage, inspire.

Discourse (noun/verb)

syn – treatise, sermon, homily, lecture, dissertation, conversation, talk, parley.

ant – reticence.

Discriminate (verb)

syn – differentiate, discern, distinguish .

ant – impartiality.

Disgrace (verb/noun)

syn – abuse, debase, degrade, demean, humble, humiliate, downgrade, insult.

ant – honour, esteem.

Disguise (verb/noun)

syn – conceal, mask, hide, cloak, veil, shroud, veneer, masquerade, pretext, pretence.

ant – reveal.

Disinterested (adjective)

syn – unaffected, dispassionate, impartial, neutral, objective, unbiased, unprejudiced, aloof, uninvolved.

ant – biased, partial.

Dismal (adjective)

syn – cheerless, depressing, dour, forbidding, grim, sombre, funereal, gloomy, melancholy, depressed, sad, doleful.

ant – cheerful, bright.

Disparate (adjective)

syn – discordant, incompatible, incongruous, absurd, heterogeneous .

ant – consistent, consonant.

Display (verb/noun)

syn – exhibition, manifestation, parade, pageant , show, open, flaunt.

ant – disguise, conceal.

Disrepute (noun)

syn – discredit, disgrace, abasement, dishonour.

ant – esteem, respect.

Disseminate (verb)

syn – advertise, blaze, blazon, broadcast, circulate, propagate, spread, promulgate, circulate, scatter, strew.

Dissent (noun/verb)

syn – clash, conflict, disharmony, confrontation, discord, dissension, strife, difference, friction, faction, schism, variance, war.

ant – assent, consent.

Dissident (noun)

syn – dissenter, heretic, nonconformist, schismatic, sectarian, separatist.

ant – supporter, follower.

Dissociate (verb)

syn – detach, disassociate, disengage, withdraw.

ant – assemble, associate.

Dissolute (adjective)

syn – abandoned, fast, dissipated, gay, uninhibited, wanton, rakish, unbridled, uncontrolled, ungoverned, licentious, wild.

ant – restrained, controlled.

Dissolve (noun/verb)

syn – fade, fadeaway, break up, fuse, liquefy, flux, crumble, disintegrate, deliquesce, decompose, melt, run, thaw.

ant – crystallize, freeze, harden.

Distaste (noun/verb)

syn – dislike, disinclination, disrelish.

ant – taste.

Distinct (adjective)

syn – apparent, clear, obvious, evident, manifest, noticeable, unmistakable, pronounced, plain, decided, definite.

ant – ambiguous, vague.

Distinguish (verb)

syn – descry, discern, make out, elevate, ennoble, spot, mark, set apart, differentiate, detect, individualize, note, observe.

ant – confuse, jumble.

Distress (noun/verb)

syn – disquietude, unease, anxiety, care, concern, solicitude, worry, anguish, torment, woe, wound, misery, trouble, hurt, injure.

ant – comfort, soothe.

Distrustful (adjective)

syn – wary, cynical, jaundiced, mistrustful, cawtious, sceptic, disillusioned.

ant – trusting, gullible.

Diverse (adjective)

syn – different, disparate, dissimilar, unlike, variant, mixed, motley, variegated, heterogeneous, miscellaneous, multifarious.

ant – none, one.

Divert (verb)

syn – amuse, entertain, recreate, regale, deter, discourage, dissuade, avert, veer, deflect, pivot, shift, swing.

ant – annoy, tire, bore.

Divide (verb/noun)

syn – allocate, allot, assign, apportion, distribute, dole out, ration, sever.

ant – unify, connect.

Dizzy (verb/adjective)

syn – fuddle, jumble, mystify, giddy, lightheaded, reeling, vertiginous, frothy, frivolous, harebrained.

Docile (adjective)

syn – amenable, submissive, tame, tractable, adaptable, compliant, obedient, malleable, yielding, tame.

ant – aggressive , stubborn.

Dodge (noun/verb)

syn – device, feint, artifice, gimmick, jig, ploy, ruse, stratagem, wile, avoid, elude, bypass, evade, subterfuge, hedge, sidestep.

ant – conform.

Dolt (noun)

syn – dummy, thickhead, dimwit, clod, chump, blockhead.

ant – sage, savant.

Domestic (adjective)

syn – familial, family, home, homely, household, internal, national, native.

ant – international, external.

Dominate (verb)

syn – rule, reign, surmount, command, prevail, predominate.

ant – submit.

Dormant (adjective)

syn – abeyant, inactive, latent, sleeping, quiescent, inactive.

ant – overt, apparent.

Doubtful (adjective)

syn – dubious, ambiguous, equivocal, uncertain, questionable, problematic, confuse, unwise, vague.

ant – certain, definite.

Downright (adjective)

syn – candid, direct, frank, honest, ingenuous, open, straight, unreserved, absolute, total, unbounded, unmitigated, thorough.

Doze (noun, verb)

syn – catnap, nap, siesta, snooze.

ant – awake.

Drab (adjective)

syn – dry, dull, arid, lifeless, flat, dim, muddy, murky, sterile, stodgy, unimaginative, aseptic.

ant – colourful, bright.

Dram (noun)

syn – ounce, shred, speck, dab, grain, dot, drop, particle, trifle, whit, jigger, tittle, shot, sip, fragment.

Drape (verb)

syn – cloak, clothe, mantle, robe, loll, sprawl, straddle, spread-eagle.

Dreadful (adjective)

syn – appalling, dire, fearsome, frightful, scary, terrible, ghastly, horrendous, awful, shocking, terrible.

ant – beautiful, appealing.

Dreary (adjective)

syn – boring, dry, dull, humdrum, irksome, tedious, monotonous, bleak, cheerless, desolate, gloomy, glum, weary, stuffy.

ant – bright, cheerful.

Drench (verb)

syn – douse, soak, sodden, sop, wet, saturate, souse.

ant – dry.

Dress (noun/verb)

syn – apparel, attire, clothes,

clothing, costume, garb, gear, togs, garment.

ant – undress, strip.

Droll (adjective)

syn – amusing, zany, comic, funny, humorous, risible, comical, laughable.

ant – tragic, somber.

Droop (verb)

syn – flop, sag, slouch, wilt, limp, flag, loll, lop.

ant – upright, stiff.

Drug (noun/verb)

syn – remedy, medicine, medicinal, pharmaceutical .

Drudge (noun/verb)

syn – slave, plod, workhorse, slog, grind.

ant – master.

Dry (noun/verb)

syn – crisp, dehydrated, dried, parched, dehumidified, desiccated .

ant – wet, damp.

Dubious (adjective)

syn – chancy, doubtful, skeptical, indeterminate, inconclusive, equivocal, dubitable, uncertain, unsure, questionable.

ant – certain, clear.

Duplicate (adjective / noun)

syn – true, identical, exact, congruent, accurate, copy.

ant – original.

E

Eager (adjective)

syn – avid, desirous, intent, keen, enthusiastic.

ant – impassive, indifferent.

Earnest (adjective)

syn – grave, sedate, serious, sober, solemn, staid, momentous.

ant – frivolous, flighty.

Ease (noun/verb)

syn – easiness, informality, naturalness, effortlessness, comfort, prosperity, mitigation, palliation, relaxation, expedite, facilitate, let up, loosen, slacken, ebb, moderate, subside, wane.

ant – agitation, nervousness.

Eat (verb)

syn – devour, dine, sup, wolf, gobble, gorge, consume, wear away, chew, swallow.

ant – starve.

Ebb (noun/verb)

syn – abatement, lessen, wane, slackening, letup, remission, draining, dwindle, recede, retract, retrogress.

ant – wax, rise.

Eccentricity (noun)

syn – oddity, quirk, idiosyncrasy, temperament, characteristic, peculiarity.

ant – normality, typicality, conventionality.

Ecclesiastic (noun)

syn – churchman, cleric, divine, minister, parson, preacher, reverend.

ant – non-conformist, radical, atheist.

Ecstasy (noun)

syn – rapture, happiness, bliss, seventh heaven.

ant – agony, torment.

Edict (noun)

syn – announcement, declaration, proclamation, manifesto, canon, decree, law, ordinance, regulation, rule.

Edge (noun/verb)

syn – border, brim, margin, rim, verge, nervous, advantage, keenness, sharpness, annoy, irritate.

ant – centre, interior.

Edit (verb)

syn – revise, amend, conduct, manage.

Educate (verb)

syn – school, teach, tutor, discipline, apprise, enlighten, acquaint, coach, instruct.

ant – neglect, ignore.

Effect (noun/verb)

syn – cause, produce, realize, result, meaning, idea, in operation, goods, bring about.

ant – cause.

Effectuate (verb)

syn – cause, bring about, induce, make, secure, trigger, effect, execute.

ant – curb, hinder.

Effervesce (verb)

syn – bubble, cream, foam fizz, froth, lather, spume, suds.

Efficient (adjective)

syn – effective, effectual, productive, industrious, efficacious.

ant – inefficient, inept.

Effort (noun)

syn – exertion, pains, struggle, trouble, attempt, labour .

ant – sloth, rest.

Effrontery (noun)

syn – churlishness, impertinence, impudence, rudeness, overbearing, contemptuous, brashness.

ant – civility, courtesy.

Effulgent (adjective)

syn – beam, bright, brilliant, irradiant, lucent, luminous, shiny, lustrous, lambent, incandescent.

ant – dull, murky.

Egregious (adjective)

syn – bad, offensive, arrant, flagrant, gross.

Egoism (noun)

syn – conceit, egotism, narcissism, self–importance, selfishness, vanity, solipsism.

ant – altruism, humility.

Eject (verb)

syn – discharge, expel, emit, oust, void, spout, reject, spew, disgorge, spurt.

ant – absorb.

Elaborate (verb/adjective)

syn – complex, involved, knotty, tangled, amplify, develop, evolve, enlarge, expand, complicated, intricate.

ant – simple, plain.

Elegant (adjective)

syn – tasteful, refined, elaborate, grandiose, ornate, sumptuous, luxurious, exquisite .

ant – vulgar, mediocre.

Elementary (adjective)

syn – basic, elemental, essential, fundamental, basal, rudimentary, beginning.

ant – advanced.

Elimination (noun)

syn – disposal, evacuation, dumping, excretion, clearance, purge, removal, eradication.

ant – inclusion, addition.

Elite (noun)

syn – chosen, best part, superior, select, clique, best.

ant – rabble.

Eloquence (noun)

syn – verbosity, expression, articulateness, wordiness.

ant – reticence, silence.

Elude (verb)

syn – evade, avoid, shun, balk, thwart, disappoint, baffle, escape.

ant – confront, face.

Embarrassment (noun)

syn – chagrin, shame, discomposure, humiliation, mortification, uncomfortable.

ant – ease, composure, temerity.

Embody (verb)

syn – comprise, involve, contain, encompass, combine, integrate, incorporate, manifest, objectify, substantiate.

Emit (verb)

syn – discharge, breathe, exhale, emanate, spurt, jet, hurt, eject, dart.

ant – absorb.

Eminence (noun)

syn – dignitary, leader, notable, personage, distinction, fame, glory, renown, prestige, illustriousness.

Emotion (noun)

syn – sentiment, feeling, affect, desire, passion, excitement, agitation.

ant – logic, rationale.

Empty (verb/adjective)

syn – discharge, vacant, evacuate, lacking, deficient, blank, bare, void, vacuous, devoid, hollow, barren, destitute, wanting.

ant – full, replete.

Enable (verb)

syn – accredit, authorize, empower, entitle, commission, permit, allow.

ant – disable, hinder.

Encompass (verb)

syn – begird, ring, have, include, consist, embrace, circle, hem, surround.

Encourage (verb)

syn – back up, embolden, foster, hearten, inspire, promote, support, help, incite, stimulate.

ant – discourage, dissuade.

Encroach (verb)

syn – infringe, intrude, invade, violate, trespass.

ant – withdraw, respect.

Endanger (verb)

syn – imperil, jeopardize, menace, risk, threaten.

ant – secure, safety.

Endorse (verb)

syn – ratify, sanction, superscribe, confirm, approve, accredit, guarantee, surety.

ant – censure, disapprove.

Engage (verb)

syn – busy, employ, book, hire, retain, interlock, mesh, encounter, meet, indulge, partake, contract, pledge, promise, monopolize, occupy, preempt.

ant – disengage, sever.

Engorgement (noun)

syn – repletion, satiation, satiety, surfeit, excess, full.

Enlarge (verb)

syn – amplify, augment, expand, increase, magnify, details.

ant – condense, shorten.

Enmity (noun)

syn – hatred, hostility, opposition, animosity, rancour, antagonism.

ant – amity, camaraderie.

Enormous (adjective)

syn – mammoth, colossal, massive, mighty, huge, behemoth, immense, vast, gigantic, tremendous, monumental, jumbo.

ant – puny, tiny.

Enrage (verb)

syn – provoke, infuriate, irritate, exasperate, inflame, chafe, excite, incense, madden, outrage.

ant – pacify, placate.

Ensign (noun)

syn – banner, symbol, sign, flag, badge, distinctive mark, standard bearer.

Enter (verb)

syn – penetrate, enroll, enjoin, embark, enlist, pierce, perforate, insert, puncture, begin, commence, record, register.

ant – depart, leave

Entertain (verb)

syn – amuse, interest, divert, receive guests, accept, consider.

ant – annoy, tire.

Enthusiasm (noun)

syn – passion, rage, mania, ardor, fervor, fire, zeal.

Entice (verb)

syn – lure, entrap, tempt, seduce, magnetize, attract, appeal, draw, inveigle, beguile.

ant – repel.

Entire (adjective)

syn – complete, full, intact, total, whole .

ant – part, partial.

Entrap (verb)

syn – catch, enmesh, ensnare, tangle, trammel, trap, web, ensnarl.

ant – release, liberate.

Entrust (verb)

syn – commit, confide, consign, delegate.

ant – distrust.

Entwine (verb)

syn – embrace, surround,

wind, twist.

ant – separate.

Enunciate (verb)

syn – pronounce, utter, say, vocalize, articulate, state.

Epistle (noun)

syn – letter, note, missive.

Equable (adjective)

syn – same, steady, changeless, constant, even, invariable, regular, uniform, unvarying.

ant – unpredictable, erratic.

Equanimity (noun)

syn – calmness, serenity, peace, unruffled, composure.

ant – agitation .

Equip (verb)

syn – furnish, outfit, supply.

ant – direst, strip.

Erase (verb)

syn – cancel, delete, efface, eradicate, expunge, obliterate.

ant – engrave, imprint.

Errant (adjective)

syn – roving, roaming, wandering, aberrant, fallible.

ant – correct, righteous.

Erode (verb)

syn – destroy, canker, corrode, eat away.

Erotic (adjective)

syn – amorous, arousing, desirous, passionate, sensual.

ant – austere.

Erudite (adjective)

syn – learned, well–read, scholarly, lettered .

ant – illiterate, unlettered.

Eruption (noun)

syn – sudden, explosion, outburst, outbreak .

Escalate (verb)

syn – increase, intensify, step up.

ant – decrease, lessen.

Escape (verb/noun)

syn – abscond, flee, fly, retreat, avoid, leave, depart, run away.

ant – surrender, confront.

Eschew (verb)

syn – avoid, shun, keep, away, from.

ant – encourage.

Essence (noun)

syn – nature, substance, extract, odour, perfume, scent, being, entity.

ant – odourless.

Essential (noun/adjective)

syn – indispensable, condition, must, necessity, need, precondition, prerequisite, necessary, basic, element, rudimentary, ultimate, integral, vital, needful, important.

ant – optional, unnecessary.

Ethereal (adjective)

syn – airy, celestial, heavenly, delicate, fragile , flimsy, tenuous, sublime.

ant – worldly, coarse.

Eulogy (noun)

syn – praise, encomium, applause, commendation, panegyric, laudation.

ant – obloquy, condemnation, criticism.

Evacuate (verb)

syn – eliminate, excrete, purge, clean out, clear, empty, vacate, void.

ant – retain, full, keep.

Everlasting (adjective/noun)

syn – endless, eternal, interminable, timeless, unending, permanent.

ant – transient, temporary, passing.

Evidence (noun)

syn – testimony, proof, attestation, voucher, manifestation.

Exaggerate (verb)

syn – magnify, inflate, hyperbolize, overcharge, overstate.

ant – understate.

Exalt (verb)

syn – raise, erect, elevate, dignify, glorify, heighten, deify.

ant – disparage, demean, insult.

Examine (verb)

syn – observe, scan, scrutinise, inspect, audit, investigate.

ant – ignore.

Excel (verb)

syn – surpass, transcend, outdo, exceed, eclipse.

ant – mediocre.

Excite (verb)

syn – arouse, evoke, stimulate, incite, impel, kindle, inflame, irritate, provoke, spur.

ant – soothe, tranquilize.

Exclude (verb)

syn – bar, preclude, reject, restrain, prevent, omit, expel, extrude, ostracise.

ant – include, admit.

Execute (verb)

syn – accomplish, enforce, effectuate, perform, do, administer.

Exemplary (adjective)

syn – ideal, scruplous, punctilious, assiduous .

ant – despicable.

Exigence (noun)

syn – demand, crisis, need, emergency, strait, extremity, juncture.

ant – unimportant.

Exile (verb)

syn – banish, deport, expatriate, relegate, rusticate, sequester .

ant – greet, welcome.

Exist (verb)

syn – occur, be, line, subsist.

ant – die.

Exonerate (verb)

syn – absolve, acquit, exculpate, vindicate.

ant – accuse, inculpate, charge, compel.

Expectation (noun)

syn – anticipation, expectancy, hope, outlook, prospect.

Expedite (verb)

syn – speed, hurry, quicken, hasten, accelerate, despatch.

ant – delay, hinder.

Expensive (adjective)

syn – dear, costly, overpriced.

ant – inexpensive, economical.

Expel (verb)

syn – banish, deport, exile, expatriate, ostracize, transport, bump, dismiss, eject, evict, oust, disgorge, erupt, spew.

ant – admit, include.

Explanation (noun)

syn – annotation, commentary, definition, description, exposition, interpretation.

ant – mystification.

Explicit (adjective)

syn – determinate, categorical, clear, plain, express, positive, obvious, apparent.

ant – implied.

Explode (verb)

syn – burst, bust, erupt.

ant – implode, absorb.

Express (verb/adjective)

syn – air, state, vent, ventilate, communicate, convey, display, phrase, depict, describe, picture, portray, articulate, say, talk, utter, verbalize, vocalize, explicit, specific.

ant – conceal.

Expunge (verb)

syn – cancel, destroy, obliterate, delete, erase, efface, wipe out.

ant – imprint.

Exquisite (adjective)

syn – fine, graceful, elegant, polished, refined.

ant – ordinary, dull, coarse.

Extempore (adverb)

syn – impromptu, without premeditation.

ant – rehearsed, prepared.

Extend (verb)

syn – stretch, widen, prolong, protract, lengthen, elongate, draw out.

ant – contract, shorten, terminate.

Extinct (adjective)

syn – asleep, dead, deceased, defunct, departed, gone, late, lifeless.

ant – existing.

Extenuate (verb)

syn – palliate, whitewash, mitigate, qualify, lessen .

ant – intensify, heighten, exaggerate.

Exterminate (verb)

syn – eliminate, uproot, destroy, abolish, eradicate.

ant – establish, repair, build.

Extol (verb)

syn – praise, laud, encomium, exalt, glorify, applaud, eulogise, panegyrise.

ant – criticise, condemn, deprecate.

Exude (verb)

syn – seep, percolate, transpire, ooze, bleed, leach, transude.

ant – absorb.

F

Fable (noun)

syn – story, fiction, tale, allegory, myth, legend, parable.

ant – fact, truth.

Facet (noun)

syn – frame of reference, regard, respect, side, angle, perspective.

Faction (noun)

syn – bloc, sect, wing, splinter group.

ant – group, whole.

Faculty (noun)

syn – capacity, ability, skill, endowment, power, privilege, ingenuity, department, profession.

ant – inability.

Fad (noun)

syn – craze, fashion, furor, mode, rage, style, trend, vogue.

ant – out-dated.

Faith (noun)

syn – belief, credence, credit, reliance, trust, church, communion, denomination, religion, sect.

Faint (adjective/noun/verb)

syn – collapse, swoon, pass out, weak, indistinct .

ant – rally, revive, come to, strong.

Fall (noun, verb)

syn – decline, drop, pitch, descent, collapse, downfall, dip, dive, plunge, spill, tumble, downswing, skid, slide, slump, topple, tumble, plummet, ebb, remit, abate, slacken, subside, surrender, wane.

ant – rise, increase.

Fallible (noun)

syn – imperfect, erring, frail, weak, ignorant .

ant – infallible, unerring.

Famous (adjective)

syn – celebrated, notorious, renowned, noted .

ant – infamous, obscure.

Fanatic (noun/adjective)

syn – enthusiast, sectary, votary, zealot, maniac, devotee, freak, extremist, radical, rabid, revolutionary, nut.

Far (adjective/adverb)

syn – distant, faraway, remote, removed, far-flung, considerably, much, quite.

ant – near close.

Farming (noun)

syn – agriculture, agrology, gardening, tillage, husbandry, agronomy.

Farthest (adjective)

syn – extreme, furthest, outermost, ultimate, utmost, uttermost.

ant – nearest, closest.

Fascinate (verb)

syn – bewitch, captivate, beguile, charm, enchant, entrance, enthrall, grip, mesmerize, rivet, spellbind, transfix.

ant – repel, aversion.

Fasten (verb)

syn – secure, join, connect, hold , unite, fix, attach, gird, bolt, chain, bind.

ant – unfasten, looser.

Fastidious (adjective)

syn – queasy, particular, finicky, precise, critical, fussy.

ant – encouraging.

Fat (noun/adjective)

syn – buxom, chubby, corpulent, obese, plump, portly, stout.

ant – thin, emaciated.

Fatal (adjective)

syn – deadly, lethal, mortal, destructive, ruinous .

ant – enlivening, invigorating.

Father (noun/verb)

syn – ancestor, forbear, parent, dad, daddy, pa, master, archetype, author, founder, creator, inventor, maker, originator, patriarch, beget, breed, engender, procreate, sire, produce.

Fathom (verb)

syn – understand, comprehend, grasp, know, get, see, sense, follow.

ant – grope.

Favourable (adjective)

syn – auspicious, fortunate, good, happy, lucky, providential, propitious.

ant – unfavorable, adverse, doomed.

Fawn (noun/verb)

syn – compliment, crawl, flatter, truckle, butter up.

ant – carp, condemn, criticise.

Fear (noun)

syn – alarm, panic, fright, horror, terror, awe, reverence.

ant – courage, bravery, equanimity.

Fecund (adjective)

syn – fertile, productive, fruitful, prolific, proliferous.

ant – sterile, barren.

Feign (verb)

syn – imagine, devise, fabricate, simulate, affect, assume, pretend, forge.

ant – sincerity, genuineness.

Feminine (adjective)

syn – female, ladylike, effeminate, womanly .

ant – masculine, manly.

Feud (noun)

syn – quarrel, enmity, vendetta, strife, contention, dissension, bickering.

ant – peace, amity.

Fey (adjective)

syn – intuitional, instinctual, theurgical, supernatural.

Fiend (noun)

syn – devil, cruel, wicked, diabolical, demoniac.

ant – angel.

Fight (noun/verb)

syn – struggle, quarrel, contest, action, battle, clash, fray, skirmish.

ant – peace, reconciliation.

Filter (verb/noun)

syn – exude, percolate, seep.

Final (adjective/noun)

syn – last, concluding, ultimate, decisive.

ant – initial, beginning.

Filch (verb)

syn – pilfer, steal, purloin, lift, swipe, pinch, snitch, heist, snatch, thieve.

Find (verb)

syn – detect, determine, discover, learn, locate, unearth, ascertain.

ant – forget, mislay, miss.

Finish (verb/noun)

syn – close, complete, conclude, end, finalise, terminate.

ant – begin, initiate, open.

Fissure (noun)

syn – cleft, rift, fracture, chasm, breach, opening, crack, crevice.

ant – complete, bridge.

Fit (verb/adjective/noun)

syn – acclimatize, accommodate, adapt, adjust, accord, agree, suit, tailor, conform, square, tally, become, befit, correspond, equip, fit out, fix, prepare, prime, furnish, gear, appropriate, proper, expedient, hale, hearty, healthy, whole, wholesome, burst, explosion, eruption, huff, passion, temper, seizure.

Flagrant (adjective)

syn – flaming, crying, notorious, raging, glowing, nefarious, wanton, monstrous.

ant – mild, venial, implicit.

Flamboyant (adjective)

syn – bright, gorgeous, ornate.

ant – plain, dull, sober.

Flare (verb)

syn – burst, erupt, explode, burn, blaze, combust, flame, blow up, anger, fume, rage, seethe, bristle.

ant – serene, tranquil.

Flash (noun/verb)

syn – gleam, glare, spark, glint, instant, moment , sparkle, twinkle, glimpse, brief, burst.

ant – dull, conceal, gloom, lacklustre.

Flaw (noun)

syn – blemish, defect, failing, fault, foible, mar, imperfection, shortcoming.

ant – merit, perfection.

Fleet (noun/adjective)

syn – armada, convoy, navy, swift, fast.

Flexible (adjective)

syn – adaptable, malleable, elastic, springy, ductile, pliable, pliant, supple, resilient, suggestible, adaptive.

ant – rigid, stiff.

Flighty (noun)

syn – wild, giddy, frivolous, fickle, light – headed, volatile.

ant – grounded, sober.

Flimsy (adjective)

syn – frail, tenuous, unsubstantial, weak.

ant – firm, rugged, solid, sturdy.

Flippant (adjective)

syn – casual, nonchalant, smart, voluble, fluent, pert, glib, trifling, talkative.

ant – solemn, serious.

Flood (noun/verb)

syn – deluge, engulf, inundate, swamp, overwhelm.

ant – drain.

Flourish (verb)

syn – flower, bloom, blossom, shine, thrive, sweep, prosper, grow.

ant – decay, decompose.

Flow (verb/noun)

syn – gush, pour, run, spout, spurt, squirt, stream.

ant – congeal, freeze, stagnate.

Fluctuate (verb)

syn – oscillate, vary, change, undulate, swing, vibrate, waver, vacillate, inconstant.

ant – stabilise, constant.

Flutter (noun)

syn – agitation, confusion, hurry, flurry, fluster, tremor, twitter, excitement.

ant – composure.

Foggy (adjective)

syn – cloudy, murky, opaque, turbid.

ant – bright, clear, sunny.

Foible (noun)

syn – frailty, failing, weakness, imperfection.

ant – forte, strength.

Follow (verb)

syn – chase, pursue, shadow, imitate, understand, obey, tag, tail, trail.

ant – lead, precede.

Folly (noun)

syn – blunder, foolishness, imbecility, absurdity, inanity, fatuity.

ant – wisdom.

Force (noun/verb)

syn – energy, might, potency, power, pressure, strength, duress, constraint, impact, impression, crew, corps, gang, team, unit, coerce, obligate, persuade.

ant – willingness, readiness.

Forego (verb)

syn – resign, renounce, cede, yield, abandon, relinquish.

ant – grab, acquire, snatch.

Foreigner (noun)

syn – alien, immigrant, newcomer, outsider, stranger .

ant – citizen, native, inhabitant.

Forget (verb)

syn – omit, neglect, overlook.

ant – remember, find.

Forgo (verb)

syn – give up, waive, sacrifice, relinquish .

ant – demand, keep, preserve.

Foreknowledge (noun)

syn – farsightedness, foresight, forethought, prescience.

ant – hindsight, ignorance.

Forerunner (noun)

syn – precursor, prelude, sign, premonition, herald, harbinger.

ant – successor, following.

Forlorn (adjective)

syn – wretched, miserable, deserted, abandoned, sad, lost, abject, desolate, disconsolate, woebegone.

ant – cheerful, warm, welcome.

Form (noun/verb)

syn – contour, shape, figure, outline, structure, kind, mould, fitness, devise, organise, arrange.

ant – destroy, vanish, lose

Formal (adjective)

syn – affected, ceremonial, pompous, proper, stiff, ritual.

ant – informal, natural, spontaneous.

Formidable (adjective)

syn – dreadful, terrible, fearful , menacing, terrific .

ant – reassuring, comforting.

Forswear (verb)

syn – renounce, deny, abjure, leave, quit, desert, abandon, recant, retract, disclaim, disown.

ant – assert, claim, retain, affirm.

Foundation (noun)

syn – basis, settlement, ground, footing, bottom, groundwork.

ant – superstructure.

Fragile (adjective)

syn – brittle , frail, frangible, friable.

ant – strong, supple, tough.

Fragrant (adjective)

syn – perfumed, scented, aromatic, odorous, balmy, ambrosial.

ant – fetid , stinking.

Fragment (noun)

syn – scrap, part, shred, iota.

ant – totality, whole.

Frantic (adjective)

syn – delirious, frenzied, frenetic, furious, hectic .

ant – tranquil, imperturbable, slow, calm.

Friend (noun)

syn – companion, comrade, crony, confidant, mate.

ant – enemy, opponent, antagonist.

Frighten (verb)

syn – scare, startle, terrify, intimidate.

ant – comfort, soothe, tranquilise, reassure.

Frigid (adjective)

syn – cold, unanimated, distant, chilling, freezing, stiff, forbidding.

ant – warm, boiling.

Frisk (verb)

syn – caper, frolic, gambol.

ant – mope, sulk.

Frown (verb)

syn – grimace, pout, scowl, disapprove.

ant – smile.

Fugitive (adjective)

syn – fleeing, escaping, transitory, flitting, unstable.

ant – permanent, stable.

Full–fledged (adjective)

syn – finished, perfected, seasoned .

ant – fledgling immature, callow.

Fundamental (adjective/noun)

syn – radical, essential, basis, principle, elementary, cardinal.

ant – secondary.

Further (adjective/adverb/verb)

syn – advance, push, contribute, implement.

ant – nearer, hinder.

Fury (noun)

syn – rage, anger, frenzy, bedlam, furore, fit.

ant – calm, placidity.

G

Gaiety (noun)

syn – glee, revelry, mirth, laughter, fun, merrymaking, hilarity, jocoseness.

ant – mourning.

Gag (verb/noun)

syn – stifle, muffle, choke, throttle.

Gallivant (verb)

syn – drift, gad, meander, ramble, range, roam, rove, stray, wander, peregrinate.

Gather (verb/noun)

syn – convene, assemble, collect, congregate, mass, muster, increase.

ant – scatter, separate, disperse.

Gauche (adjective)

syn – boorish, maladroit, tactless, uncouth, unpolished.

ant – urbane, sophisticated.

Gambol (verb)

syn – caper, cavort, dance, frisk, frolic, rollick, romp.

Gape (noun/verb)

syn – gaze, stare, see, eye, gawk, gaze, ogle, peer, goggle.

Garish (adjective)

syn – flashy, glaring, loud, tawdry, gaudy, meretricious.

Garrulous (adjective)

syn – chatty, conversational, talkative, voluble, loquacious.

ant – reticent, silent.

Gaudy (adjective)

syn – flashy, garish, tawdry,

meretricious, cheap, showy, ostentatious.

ant – simple, tasteful, plain.

Gaunt (adjective)

syn – lean, thin, emaciated, lanky, haggard.

ant – plump, corpulent.

Gelid (adjective)

syn – arctic, frosty, glacial, icy, polar, wintry, frigid, freezing.

ant – boiling, steaming, hot.

Gem (noun)

syn – jewel, rock, stone, jewellery, precious.

General (adjective/noun)

syn – accepted, common, popular, public, universal, vague, inexact.

ant – specific, queer, unusual, rare, precise.

Generous (adjective)

syn – bountiful, lavish, liberal, magnanimous.

ant – mean, greedy, parsimonious.

Genius (noun/adjective)

syn – aptitude, bent, faculty, gift, instinct, knack, talent, intelligent, exceptionally, gifted.

ant – moron, dunce, blockhead.

Genuflection (noun)

syn – bow, curtsy, nod, kowtow, obeisance.

Genuine (adjective)

syn – actual, authentic, real, true, veritable, unaffected, sincere.

ant – spurious, false, superficial, fake.

Get (verb)

syn – acquire, gain, obtain, procure, fetch, bring, cause, become, reach.

ant – give, lose, relinquish.

Ghost (noun)

syn – spectre, spirit, spook, wraith, phantom, apparition, shade.

Giant (noun/adjective)

syn – behemoth, goliath, jumbo, titan, mammoth, immense, colossal, massive, heroic, mighty, enormous, huge, vast, tremendous.

ant – puny, tiny, dwarfish.

Give (verb)

syn – provide, accord,

award, cause, submit, present, confer, grant.

ant – take, withdraw.

Glean (verb)

syn – cull, extract, garner, gather, collect.

Gloomy (adjective)

syn – dark, dreary, grey, murky, sombre.

ant – bright, cheerful.

Glower (verb)

syn – stare, glare, scowl, look fierce.

ant – smile, cheer.

Gnash (verb)

syn – bite, champ, chomp, gnaw, crunch, grind.

Go (verb)

syn – advance, move, proceed, progress, rise, depart.

ant – come, stop.

Goodness (noun)

syn – morality, integrity, probity, purity, virtue, rectitude, righteousness.

ant – badness, depravity, evil.

Gorge (noun/verb)

syn – ravine, devour, swallow, throat, glut.

ant – fast, starve.

Gourmet (noun)

syn – epicure, glutton, gastronome, greedy, gourmand.

Grace (noun/verb)

syn – altruism, benevolence, charity, kindness, goodwill, elegance, polish, favour, indulgence, charity, clemency, benediction, mercy, enhance, adorn, embellish.

ant – coarseness, disgrace.

Grandiloquent (adjective)

syn – bombastic, rhetorical, verbose, pompous.

ant – precise, reticent.

Graphic (adjective)

syn – pictorial, vivid, picturesque.

ant – unclear.

Grasp (verb)

syn – understand, clasp, grab, grip, seize, snatch, clutch.

ant – release, abandon.

Grateful (adjective)

syn – appreciative, thankful.

ant – indifferent, ungrateful.

Grave (noun/adjective/verb)

syn – crypt, tomb, vault,

cenotaph, sepulchre, mausoleum, serious, carve.

ant – frivolous, trivial.

Great (adjective)

syn – eminent, large, remarkable, important, illustrious, reputable, notable, noteworthy.

ant – obscure, unknown, small, slight, minor.

Greedy (adjective)

syn – acquisitive, avaricious, covetous, envious, gluttonous, stingy, rapacious.

ant – generous, selfless.

Greet (verb)

syn – accost, address, hail, salute, welcome.

ant – ignore.

Gregarious (adjective)

syn – sociable, friendly, affable, cordial, outgoing, social, amiable.

ant – introverted, aloof, reserved, reclusive.

Grieve (verb)

syn – lament, mourn, sorrow.

ant – exult, jubiliate, rejoice.

Grimace (noun)

syn – smirk, mow, mop, frown, wry face.

ant – smile.

Grind (verb/noun)

syn – crush, gnash, masticate, chomp, chew.

Grouchy (adjective)

syn – sulky, sullen, surly, morose, crabbed, glum, moody.

ant – cheerful, lively, bubbly.

Group (noun/verb)

syn – band, body, company, gang, party, troop, troupe.

ant – fragment, individual.

Grovel (verb)

syn – cringe, fawn, toady, truckle, bootlick.

Grudge (verb/noun)

syn – envy, reluctance, ill – will, spite, malice, enmity, rancour, resentment, malevolence.

ant – affection, goodwill.

Gruesome (adjective)

syn – morbid, macabre, ghastly, grim, grisly, lurid, hideous.

ant – delightful, pleasing.

Guide (verb/noun)

syn – conduct, advise, direct, read, navigate, pilot, steer.

ant – misguide, mislead.

Guile (noun)

syn – deceit, cunning, craft, duplicity.

ant – candour, sincerity, honesty.

Gullible (adjective)

syn – credulous, naïve, trusting, unsuspicious .

ant – sceptical, critical.

Gush (noun/verb)

syn – spout, spurt, sentimental, emotional.

ant – drip.

Gut (noun/adjective)

syn – bravery, gallantry, courage, nerve, pluck, valiant, spunk, valour, inner, internal, inward, visceral, mettle.

Guttural (adjective)

syn – gruff, hoarse, throaty, thick.

ant – soprano.

H

Habitat (noun)

syn – locality, area, surroundings.

Habitual (adjective)

syn – accustomed, chronic, routine, usual.

ant – unaccustomed.

Hallow (verb)

syn – consecrate, reverence, venerate, sanctify, make holy, respect.

ant – desecrate, defile.

Handy (adjective)

syn – dexterous, skilful, expert, adroit, skilled.

ant – inconvenient, clumsy.

Happen (verb)

syn – befall, occur, transpire, chance, take place.

Happiness (noun)

syn – joy, gladness, bliss, felicity, beatitude, pleasure.

ant – unhappiness, grief, misery, sorrow.

Hard (adjective/ adverb)

syn – firm, solid, difficult, arduous, laborious, trying, perplexing, troublesome, hostile, indisputable, fixed, heavily, severely.

ant – easy, soft, simple, tender.

Harangue (noun/verb)

syn – speech, tirade, address publicly, ranting, declaim.

ant – quiet, reticence.

Harm (noun/verb)

syn – damage, disable, hurt,

injure, incapacitate .

ant – repair, treat, benefit.

Harmonise (verb)

syn – unite, adapt, synchronise, attune, reconcile, accord, correspond, blend, tally, conform.

ant – discordant, differ.

Haste (noun, verb)

syn – hastiness, rush, rashness, celerity, fleetness, tearing hurry, bolt, bustle, flash, speediness, swiftness, run, rocket, scout, dispatch, rush, sail, scoot, zip, zoom.

ant – leisure.

Hauteur (noun)

syn – arrogance, disdain, pride, contempt, haughtiness, snobbish.

ant – humility, modesty.

Havoc (noun)

syn – ravage, desolation, ruin, carnage, waste, destruction, devastation.

ant – prosperity.

Hazard (noun/verb)

syn – accident, chance, fluke, hap, fortuity, luck, danger, peril, jeopardy, risk.

ant – safety, security.

Headstrong (adjective)

syn – obstinate, stubborn, unruly, dogged, intractable, cantankerous .

ant – adaptable, tractable, prudent.

Healthy (adjective)

syn – fit, hale, hearty, robust, sound, strong, vigorous, well.

ant – sick, unhealthy.

Heathen (noun)

syn – barbarian, gentile, infidel, pagan, heretic, renegade, sceptic.

ant – godly, believer, religious

Heavy (adjective/noun)

syn – burdensome, onerous, oppressive, crushing .

ant – light, mild.

Heedless (adjective)

syn – careless, incautious, insensitive, thoughtless, inconsiderate, reckless, rash, precipitate.

ant – heedful, considerate.

Help (verb/noun)

syn – aid, assistance, succour, relief, service, support.

ant – harm, hinder.

Herculean (adjective)

syn – strong, powerful, mighty, muscular, sinewy, strapping, gigantic, colossal.

ant – puny, weakling.

Heretic (noun)

syn – dissenter, non-conformist, schismatic, sectarian.

ant – adherent, conformist, supporter, orthodox.

Hesitate (verb)

syn – pause, falter, demur, flounder, waver, vacillate, delay, doubt.

ant – decide, choose, ascertain, assert.

Heterogeneous (adjective)

syn – mixed, motley, miscellaneous, diverse, indiscriminate.

ant – homogeneous, uniform.

Hew (verb)

syn – chop, cut, hack, sever.

ant – adjoin.

Hiatus (noun)

syn – break, void, lacuna, gap, interim.

ant – continue.

High (adjective/adverb)

syn – tall, elevated, advanced, lofty, towering.

ant – low, base.

Hilarious (adjective)

syn – gay, jovial, jolly, merry, mirthful, funny.

ant – gloomy, morbid, serious.

Hinder (verb/adjective)

syn – hamper, impede, obstruct, encumber.

ant – impel, spur, encourage, help.

Hint (noun/verb)

syn – implication, innuendo, insinuation, intimation, suggestion.

ant – declaration, affirmation.

Hire (verb/noun)

syn – conscript, employ, engage, enlist, recruit.

ant – fire, retire, discharge.

Hobby (noun)

syn – sport, recreation, pastime, avocation.

ant – profession, business.

Hole (noun/verb)

syn – cavity, hollow, pit, excavation.

ant – protrusion.

Home (noun/adverb/verb)

syn – abode, domicile, habitation, residence, household, house, lodging, dwelling.

ant – foreign.

Honorable (adjective)

syn – admirable, deserving, estimable, laudable, reputable, respectable, good, honest, true, upright, righteous, worthy.

ant – dishonorable, corrupt.

Hope (verb/noun)

syn – anticipate, expect, await, dream, foresee, wish.

ant – despair, hopelessness.

Horrendous (adjective)

syn – appalling, awful, dreadful, frightful, ghastly, horrible, shocking, terrible.

ant – admirable.

Hostility (noun)

syn – enmity, animosity, antagonism, ill–will, repugnance.

ant – friendliness, amity.

Hot (adjective)

syn – burning, feverish, scorching, searing, sizzling, sultry, torrid.

ant – cold, cool.

Hotel (noun)

syn – pub, tavern, guest house, inn, motel, boarding house.

Hubbub (noun)

syn – clamour, din, confusion, disorder, uproar, outcry.

ant – silence, calm, tranquility.

Humane (adjective)

syn – benign, charitable, compassionate, humanitarian, philanthropic.

ant – cruel, barbarian, beastly.

Humdrum (adjective)

syn – dull, dreary, monotonous, tedious, wearisome.

ant – unusual, interesting.

Humid (adjective)

syn – sticky, oppressive, sultry.

ant – arid, dry, parched.

Humorous (adjective)

syn – comic, droll, funny, jocose, jocular, witty, facetious.

ant – serious, gloomy, dull.

Hunt (verb)

syn – explore, scour, search, seek, sleuth, ransack.

ant – find, discover.

Hurl (verb)

syn – throw, fling, cast, pitch, dart, whirl.

ant – catch.

Husky (adjective/ noun)

syn – beefy, brawny, burly, stocky, hulking, strapping, breed of dog, hoarse.

ant – thin, frail, emaciated.

Hypnotic (adjective/ noun)

syn – mesmeric, opiate, somniferous, soporific.

Hypocrite (noun)

syn – deceiver, insincere, pretender, cheat.

ant – genuine, sincere.

Hygienic (adjective)

syn – healthy, wholesome, salubrious, healthful, salutary.

ant – dirty, unhygienic.

Hyperbole (noun)

syn – exaggeration, overstatement, tall talk.

ant – understate.

Hypothetical (adjective)

syn – conjectural, inferential, supposed, presumptive, theoretical.

ant – factual, real.

I

Idea (noun)

syn – belief, opinion, concept, plans, meaning, notion, thought, conception, impression.

ant – fact, reality.

Identical (adjective)

syn – same, equivalent, ditto, tantamount, alike.

ant – different, unlike.

Idle (adjective)

syn – inactive, inert, lazy, slothful, free, indolent, ineffectual, trivial, trifling, unprofitable.

ant – active, busy.

Ignoble (adjective)

syn – base, cheap, low, mean, shabby, contemptible.

ant – moral, noble.

Ignorant (adjective)

syn – uninformed, unread, unenlightened, illiterate, unaware, untaught.

ant – aware, learned.

Ill (adjective/noun/adverb)

syn – bad, evil, unwell, faulty, wicked, wrong, harmful, sick, ailing, diseased, surly, peevish, hateful, malevolent, ugly, badly, calamity, harm, with difficulty.

ant – well, good.

Imagination (noun)

syn – fancy, fantasy, reverie, illusion, notion.

ant – actuality, fact, reality, truth.

Image (noun/verb)

syn – statue, idol, likeness, picture, form, symbol, reflection, embodiment, resemblance.

Imbibe (verb)

syn – absorb, assimilate, receive, gather, acquire, gain, drink, suck.

ant – eject, reject.

Imitate (verb)

syn – ape, copy, mimic, impersonate, duplicate, forge, reproduce, mirror, echo, travesty, burlesque.

ant – create, original.

Immaculate (adjective)

syn – spotless, stainless, undefiled, untainted, clean, unsullied, pure, perfect.

ant – impure, stained, tainted.

Immature (noun)

syn – unripe, raw, unformed, undeveloped, premature, hasty, youthful, childish.

ant – mature, experienced, seasoned, veteran.

Immediate (adjective)

syn – close, near, next, direct, unmediated, instant, prompt.

ant – distant, future.

Immense (adjective)

syn – infinite, boundless, unbounded, huge, vast, enormous, gigantic, colossal, large, mountainous, infinite.

ant – puny, tiny, small.

Immerse (verb)

syn – dip, plunge, sink, douse, bathe, engage, absorb.

ant – extract, eject.

Imminent (adjective)

syn – threatening, harm, alarming, impending, near at hand, perilous, overhanging.

ant – past, retrospect.

Immobile (adjective)

syn – fixed, motionless, steadfast, stable, rigid, stiff, dull, stolid, expressionless, impassive.

ant – mobile, movable, flexible.

Immodest (adjective)

syn – indelicate, crude, gross, coarse, loud, obscene, bold, brazen, indecent.

ant – modest, decorous, bashful.

Immoral (adjective)

syn – unethical, wicked, depraved, dissolute, indecent, sinful, corrupt, unprincipled.

ant – moral, ethical.

Immortal (adjective)

syn – undying, deathless, imperishable, immutable, infinite, permanent.

ant – mortal, temporary, perishable.

Immutable (adjective)

syn – fixed, indestructible, unchangeable, unfading, unvarying, unchanging.

ant – changeable, inconstant, temporary.

Impact (noun/verb)

syn – shock, touch, impulse, collision, wedge, brunt, concussion, jolt, force.

ant – cushion.

Impassioned (adjective)

syn – fervid, fervent, zealous, warm, ardent, vehement, glowing, passionate, intense.

ant – cool, tepid.

Impassive (adjective)

syn - apathetic, stolid, indifferent, expressionless, poker faced.

ant – responsive

Impatient (adjective)

syn – uneasy, restless, eager, impetuous, hasty, intolerant, hot, violent, fretful, irritable.

ant – patient, tolerant

Impel (verb)

syn – drive, push, urge, send, press, induce, prod persuade, instigate, incite, stimulate, compel.

ant – inhibit, quell, prevent.

Impertinence (noun)

syn – impudence, insolence, sauciness, pertness, rudeness, effrontery, impropriety.

ant – courtesy, politeness

Imperturable (adjective)

syn – calm, composed, collected, sober, dispassionate serene, unmoved, placid, trandquil, sedate.

ant – agitated, excited, volatile.

Impetuous (adjective)

syn – headstrong, impulsive, precipitate, sudden, heedless, reckless.

ant – cautious, prudent.

Implant (verb)

syn – plant, fix, imbue, infuse, inculcate, ingrain, instil.

ant – uproot.

Implicit (adjective)

syn – covert, implied, inferred, tacit, unspoken, latent, potential, unshaken, steadfast, firm.

ant – overt, definite, obvious.

Important (adjective)

syn – weighty, significant, valuable, grave, urgent, considerable, prominent, influential, serious, esteemed, pompous, consequential.

ant – unimportant, inconsequential.

Impostor (noun)

syn – deceiver, cheat, rogue, trickster, knave, hypocrite, pretender.

ant – genuine, honest.

Impotence (noun)

syn – disability, weakness, incompetence, feebleness, frailty, inability, weakness of procreative power.

ant – virility, strength.

Impregnable (adjective)

syn – invincible, unconquerable, invulnerable, unassailable, inexpungable.

ant – conquerable.

Impress (verb/noun)

syn – stamp, print, fix, imprint, seal, motto, symbol, emblem, mark, strike, affect, move.

ant – ignore.

Improper (adjective)

syn – unsuitable, unfit, right, inappropriate, wrong, unseemly, indecent, inaccurate, erroneous, incorrect.

ant – proper, suited, apt.

Impropriety (noun)

syn – unseemliness, inaccuracy, incorrectness, indecorum, unfitness, inappropriateness.

ant – propriety, decorous.

Improve (verb)

syn – better, ameliorate, amend, rectify, correct, edify, mend, rise, become enhanced.

ant – worsen, deteriorate

Impudence (noun)

syn – check, impertinence, sauciness, pertness, gall,

audacity,boldness, insolence.

ant – politeness, courtesy.

Impulse (noun)

syn – push, impetus, momentum, instinct, gut feeling, proclivity, instigation.

ant – logic, reasoning.

Inactive (adjective)

syn – inert, idle, quiet, dormant, indolent, supine, slothful, lifeless, dull, sluggish.

ant – active, busy.

Inborn (adjective)

syn – innate, inherent, inbred, ingrained, natural.

ant – acquired, learnt.

Incense (verb/noun)

syn – enrage, inflame, anger, chafe, perfume, madden, heat, excite, exasperate.

ant – pacify, mollify, calm.

Incite (verb)

syn – arouse, exhort, forment, instigate, provoke, rouse, stir up.

ant – subdue, discourage, deter.

Inclement (adjective)

syn – severe, unmerciful, harsh, boisterous, rigorous, cruel, stormy.

ant – clement, mild, kind.

Incline (verb)

syn – lean, slope, slant, verge, bend, bow, feel desire for, proclivity, bias, predisposition.

ant – repel, aversion.

Include (verb)

syn – comprise, contain, involve, possess.

ant – exclude, omit, leave out.

Incongruous (adjective)

syn – inconsistent, unfit, inappropriate, absurd, contrary, incompatible.

ant – congruous.

Inconsiderate (adjective)

syn – unthoughtful, heedless, indifferent, intolerant rash, hasty, careless, negligent.

ant – considerate, heedful.

Inconstant (adjective)

syn – capricious, changeable, erratic, fickle, variable, varying, mercurial.

ant – constant, steadfast, fixed.

Incontrovertible (adjective)

syn – certain, hard, inarguable, incontestable, irrefutable, positive, sure, undeniable.

ant – controversial, disputed.

Inconvenient (adjective)

syn – difficult, incommodious, troublesome, untimely, inopportune, inaccessible.

ant – convenient, timely.

Incorrect (adjective)

syn – erroneous, false, inaccurate, mistaken, unsound, untrue, wrong.

ant – correct.

Incorrigible (adjective)

syn – irremediable, irreversible, irrecoverable, incurable, hopeless, hardened, beyond help.

ant – corrigible, reformable.

Increase (noun/verb)

syn – aggrandizement, amplification, boost, enlargement, growth, raise, multiplication, swell, upsurge, rise, augment, escalate, expand, soar, proliferate, breed.

ant – decrease, decline.

Incriminate (verb)

syn – accuse, arraign, charge, denounce, indict, implicate, inculpate.

Inculcate (verb)

syn – drill, drive, implant, impress, instill, indoctrinate.

Incur (verb)

syn – assume, shoulder, tackle, take on, take over, accept.

Indecent (adjective)

syn – indecorous, improper, unbecoming, unseemly, offensive, bold, outrageous, indelicate, gross, coarse, obscene, lewd, filthy, unchaste.

ant – decent, pure, chaste, moral.

Indeed (adverb)

syn – truly, really, veritable, verily, stricty, positively, certainly, absolutely.

Indefatigable (adjective)

syn – tireless, inexhaustible, unfailing, unflagging, untiring, unwearied.

ant – tired, exhausted, fatigued.

Indent (noun)

syn – impress, impression, imprint, mark, print, stamp.

Index (noun)

syn – badge, note, evidence, indication, manifestation, sign, token, witness.

Indicate (verb)

syn – show, denote, tell, register, manifest, presage specify, suggest, imply, hint, intimate, mar

ant – conceal.

Indifference (noun)

syn – apathy, impassiveness, lassitude, lethargy, unconcern, inconsequence, insignificance.

ant – concern, care, love.

Indigent (adjective)

syn – poor, destitute, needy, penniless, insolvent, destitute.

ant – moneyed, wealthy.

Indignity (noun)

syn – insult, affront, outrage, disrespect, abuse, reproach, opprobrium.

ant – dignity, respect.

Indiscreet (adjective)

syn – ill-advised, impolitic, imprudent, injudicious, unsound, unwise.

ant – wise, discreet.

Indistinct (adjective)

syn – bleary, cloudy, dim, faint, foggy, fuzzy, hazy, indefinite, misty, obscure, shadowy, vague.

ant – distinct, clear, obvious, apparent.

Indocile (adjective)

syn – disorderly, fractious, intractable, recalcitrant, lawless, obstinate, untoward, ungovernable, wild.

ant – docile, obedient.

Induce (verb)

syn – coax, cajole, urge, wheedle, persuade, impel, incite, spur, cause, produce, lead, effect, entire, allure, prompt, motivate.

ant – discourage, repel, subdue.

Induct (verb)

syn – conscript, draft, levy, inaugurate, initiate, install, instate.

ant – terminate, fire, discard.

Indulge (verb)

syn – gratify, satisfy,

humour, cosset, coddle, yield, pamper, allow, cherish, wallow.

ant – deny.

Industrious (adjective)

syn – diligent, assiduous, laborious, brisk, sedulous, persistent, persevering.

ant – slothful, inactive.

Inebriate (noun/adjective)

syn – drunk, sot, tippler, intoxicated, plastered, stoned.

ant – sober, teetotaller.

Inept (adjective)

syn – unfit, awkward, useless, worthless, void, null, foolish, silly, stupid, nonsensical.

ant – competent, apt.

Inequity (noun)

syn – iniquity, injustice, wrong, disservice.

Inert (adjective)

syn – lifeless, comatose, dead, passive, motionless, dull, lazy, idle, supine, sluggish indolent.

ant – active, lively, animate.

Inevitable (adjective)

syn – inescapable, unavoidable, necessary.

ant – avertible, optional.

Inexorable (adjective)

syn – merciless, pitiless, relentless, remorseless, ruthless, unrelenting.

ant – placable, yielding, clement.

Inexpensive (adjective)

syn – cheap, low-priced, modest

ant – expensive.

Inexperienced (adjective)

syn – green, raw, inexpert, uninitiated, unpracticed, untried.

ant – experienced, seasoned.

Inexplicit (adjective)

syn – ambiguous, cloudy, equivocal, obscure, uncertain, unclear, vague.

ant – certain, clear.

Infamy (noun)

syn – disgracefulness, shamefulness, notoriety, ignominy.

ant – fame, renown.

Infatuate (verb)

syn – besot, delude, befool,

stultify, captivate, attract.

ant – repulse, dislike.

Infect (verb)

syn – canker, poison, corrupt, defile, pollute, contaminate, soil, taint.

ant – clean

Infer (verb)

syn – deduce, conclude, gather, draw, reason, glean, guess, presume, assume.

ant – knowledge.

Infiltrate (verb)

syn – edge, foist, wind, work, worm, insinuate.

Infinite (adjective)

syn – boundless, limitless, countless.

ant – finite, counted, limited.

Infirm (adjective)

syn – decrepit, puny, delicate, weak, tottery, shaky, unwell, feeble, frail.

ant – strong, healthy.

Inflame (verb)

syn – burn, irritate, sting, excite, foment, goad, impel, incite, inspire, pique, prick, prod, propel, spur, instigate.

ant – soothe, calm, extinguish.

Inflict (verb)

syn – foist, impose, saddle, play, visit.

Influence (noun)

syn – affect, impress, sway.

ant – subdue, discourage.

Inform (verb)

syn – advise, apprise, acquaint, notify, enlighten.

ant – misinform, withold.

Infringe (verb)

syn – break, violate, transgress, encroach, trespass, intrude.

Infuriate (verb)

syn – anger, enrage, incense, madden, provoke, burn up.

ant – excite, cheer.

Ingenious (adjective)

syn – gifted, intelligent, clever, artful, skilled, adroit, shrewd, witty.

ant – foolish, stupid.

Ingest (verb)

syn – consume, devour, eat, fare, partake, swallow.

Ingress (noun)

syn – access, admission, entrance, entry.

ant – departure, exit.

Inhabit (verb)

syn – occupy, people, populate.

Inherent (adjective)

syn – essential, innate, intrinsic, native, inborn, ingrained, adhering.

ant – extraneous, overt.

Inhuman (adjective)

syn – barbaric, bestial, cruel, feral, fierce, savage, vicious, wolfish.

ant – humane, kind.

Inimical (adjective)

syn – hostile, unfriendly.

ant – friendly, cordial, warm.

Initiative (noun)

syn – drive, enterprise, hustle, punch, gumption, push.

Inject (verb)

syn – insert, interject, interlard, interpolate, interpose, introduce.

Injudicious (adjective)

syn – unwise, indiscreet, foolish, rash, hasty, incautious, imprudent, ill-advised.

ant – judicious, prudent.

Injurious (adjective)

syn – bad, deleterious, evil, harmful, hurtful, ill, defamatory, scandalous, invidious.

Inkling (noun)

syn – hint, implication, suspicion, undercurrent, undertone.

ant – obvious, loud, apparent.

Innate (adjective)

syn – congenital, hereditary, inborn, inbred.

ant – acquired, learnt.

Inner (adjective)

syn – interior, inward, internal

ant – outer, exterior, external.

Innocent (adjective)

syn – blameless, guiltless, irreproachable, sinless, untainted, moral, chaste, good.

ant – guilty, immoral.

Inoperative (adjective)

syn – idle, inactive, inert.

ant – operative, active, working.

Inopportune (adjective)

syn – ill-timed, inconvenient, untimely.

ant – propitious, favorable.

Inquiry (noun)

syn – probe, study, inquest, inquisition, enquiry, examination.

Insalubrious (adjective)

syn – unhealthy, unwholesome, unsalutary.

ant – healthy, salubrious.

Insecure (adjective)

syn – unguarded, unsafe, unprotected, infirm, shaky, tottering, unsteady, unsure, weak, precarious.

ant – secure, strong, firm.

Insert (verb)

syn – interject, interpolate, interpose, introduce.

ant – extract, remove, detach.

Insidious (adjective)

syn – sly, artful, crafty, cunning, deceitful, tricky.

ant – straightforward, honest.

Insinuate (verb)

syn – hint, suggest, intimate, infuse, instil

ant – declare, assert.

Insipid (adjective)

syn – tasteless, bland, boring, uninteresting, stale, flat, vapid, tame, dull.

ant – spicy, interesting.

Insolence (noun)

syn – rudeness, contempt, disrespect, impertinence pertness, insult, insubordination.

ant – deference, regard.

Insolvent (adjective)

syn – bankrupt, broke, impecunious.

ant – solvent, prosperous, wealthy.

Insular (adjective)

syn – narrow, island-like, contracted, petty, isolated, remote, prejudiced.

ant – impartial, broad-minded.

Intelligent (adjective)

syn – astute, sensible, shrewd, clever, discerning, alert, sagacious.

ant – stupid, moron.

Intend (verb)

syn – aim, plan, mean, propose, contemplate, try.

ant – act.

Integrity (noun)

syn – wholeness, probity,

honesty, uprightness, principled, virtue, moral soundness.

ant – dishonesty, corrupted.

Interim (noun)

syn – interval, meantime, intermediate, bull.

Intimidate (verb)

syn – bully, browbeat, daunt, frighten, dismay, overawe, terrorize.

ant – encourage, comfort.

Intuition (noun)

syn – instinct, gut feeling, divination, insight, presentiment.

ant – logic, reasoning.

Invalid (adjective/noun)

syn – sick, infirm, unwell, ailing, feeble, void, null, unsound, baseless, untrue.

ant – valid, hearty, healthy.

Inveigle (verb)

syn – beguile, ensnare, lure, entrap, cajole, entice.

ant – repel, avoid.

Invoke (verb)

syn – implore, entreat, solicit, pray, supplicate beseech, call upon, request.

ant – command, order

Ire (noun)

syn – wrath, anger, rage, fury, indignation.

ant – composure, calm.

Irrelevant (adjective)

syn – inapplicable, unrelated, inconsequent, foreign, impertinent, extraneous, illogical.

ant – relevant, pertinent.

J

Jabber (verb)

syn – prattle, talk, chatter, gabble, idle chat.

ant – reticence.

Jargon (noun)

syn – slang, rigmarole lingo, cant, argot, gabble.

Jarring (adjective)

syn – raspy, grating, dry, harsh, hoarse, raucous, rough, scratchy, squawky, strident.

ant – soothing, calming.

Jaunty (adjective)

syn – chirpy, debonair, insouciant, sprightly, gay.

ant – sedate, serious.

Jealous (adjective)

syn – covetous, invidious, clutching, envious, possessive.

Jeer (noun/verb)

syn – gibe, scoff, insult, taunt, twit, deride, jest, laugh, mock, ridicule.

ant – sober, serious, respect.

Jell (verb)

syn – clot, coagulate, congeal, curdle, jelly, gelatinize.

ant – liquefy.

Jeopardy (noun)

syn – danger, hazard, peril, risk, venture.

ant – protection, safeguard, safety.

Jest (noun/verb)

syn – joke, mockery, derision, gag, quip, witticism, scoff, twit.

ant – earnestness, seriousness.

Jibe (verb)

syn – accord, agree, check, consist, correspond, fit, match, harmonize.

ant – incongruous, discordant.

Jittery (adjective)

syn – edgy, fidgety, jumpy, nervous, restive, tense, skittish.

ant – calm, serene.

Jocund (adjective)

syn – merry, gay, jovial, blithe, jolly, lively, joyful, cheerful, debonair, jocose.

ant – serious, melancholy, gloomy.

Jog (noun/verb)

syn – dig, jab, nudge, poke, lope trot.

ant – dawdle, amble.

Joke (noun)

syn – gag, jest, quip, wisecrack, pleasantry, witticism, ridicule, caricature.

ant – serious.

Jolt (noun/verb)

syn – bump, collision, crash, impact, jar, shock, smash, percussion, bump, jerk, electrify, startle.

ant – steady.

Jostle (verb)

syn – strike, hit, shake, shove, hustle, shoulder, collide.

Journey (noun)

syn – jaunt, excursion, tour, trip, voyage.

Joyous (adjective)

syn – esctatic, elated, glad, euphoric, happy, high

ant – morose, sad, gloomy.

Juncture (noun)

syn – crisis, crossroad, pass, turn, turning point, instant, point, connection, coupling, joint, junction, seam, union.

Junket (noun verb)

syn – feast, delicacy, banquet, pudding, entertain.

Jurisdiction (noun)

syn – authority, power, sovereignty, sway, judicature, control, legal power, range.

Justify (verb)

syn – vindicate, acquit, absolve, exonerate, defend, exculpate, excuse, clear from guilt.

ant – accuse, charge.

Juvenile (adjective)

syn – immature, childish, youthful, puerile.

ant – seasoned, mature.

Juxtaposition (noun)

syn – nearness, contact, adjacency, proximity

ant – distant, remote.

K 

Kaput (adjective)

syn – done for, finished, through, washed up.

Keen (adjective)

syn – eager, ardent, zealous, sharp, acute, severe, shrewd, astute, penetrating, earnest.

ant – languid, bland, apathetic.

Keep (noun/verb)

syn – retain, hold, execute, exercise, fulfill, implement, perform, maintain, last, adhere, rein, withhold, brake, check, constraint, curb, inhibit, support, reserve, put by.

ant – discard, destroy.

Keeper (noun)

syn – caretaker, custodian, guardian, conservator.

Keepsake (noun)

syn – memento, remembrance, reminder, token, trophy, souvenir.

Ken (noun/verb)

syn – horizon, purview, range, reach, scope, apprehend, compass, comprehend, fathom, grasp, know, understand.

Kernel (noun)

syn – crux, gist, essence, nub, nucleus, substance.

ant – periphery, perimeter, shell.

Key (noun/adjective)

syn – formula, route, secret, central, pivotal, major, capital, cardinal, chief, first, foremost, main, prime, principal.

ant – secondary.

Kick (noun/verb)

syn – gripe, grouse, whine, complaint, grievance, bang boot, break, cut out, give up, object, challenge, demur, expostulate, remonstrate.

ant – support, endorse.

Kid (noun/verb)

syn – child, innocent, juvenile, moppet, youngster, banter, chaff, joke, rib, rag

Kidnap (verb)

syn – abduct, snatch, spirit away.

ant – restore, return.

Kill (verb)

syn – assassinate, butcher, dispatch, execute, murder, massacre, slaughter, slay.

ant – enliven, create.

Kin (noun)

syn – family, kindred, kinsfolk, kinsmen, relations, relatives.

Kind (adjective/noun)

syn – altruistic, beneficent, benevolent, benign, good, kindhearted, breed, cast, description, feather, ilk, lot, species, type, variety.

Kindle (verb)

syn – light, inflame, ignite, incite, rouse, whet, provoke, stimulate, thrill, stir, fire.

ant – extinguish, douse, quell.

Kindred (adjective/noun)

syn – affinity, relationship, related, congenial, sympathetic, consanguinity, cognate.

ant – unrelated.

Kiss (noun/verb)

syn – smacker, peck, brush, flick, graze, osculate.

Knack (noun)

syn – ability, art, adeptness, command, craft, expertise, expertness, mastery, skill, proficiency, technique, bent, faculty, flair, talent, head, instinct, genius.

ant – ineptitude.

Knead (verb)

syn – manipulate, work, mix, form, shape.

Knell (verb)

syn – bong, peal, ring, strike, toll, chime.

Knife (noun)

syn – dagger, poniard, stiletto.

Knob (noun)

syn – bulge, jut, knot, projection, protrusion, bump, hump, lump.

Knockabout (adjective)

syn – rough, rough-and-tumble, rugged, tough, strenuous.

Knot (noun/verb)

syn – bond, ligament, link, tie, yoke, bulge, jut, knob, projection, array, bevy, body, entanglement, maze, labyrinth, mesh, bind, fasten, web, secure, tie.

ant – untie, unfasten.

Know (verb)

syn – discern, differentiate, distinguish, tell, experience, feel, have, meet, see, suffer, have, apprehend, comprehend, fathom, grasp, understand.

ant – ignore, oversight.

Knowledge (noun)

syn – comprehension, learning, erudition, wit, discernment, lore, information, mastery, cognizance, prescience, cognition.

ant – ignorance.

Kowtow (noun/verb)

syn – bow, nod, curtsy, genuflection, obeisance, cringe, fawn, toady, truckle.

Kook (noun)

syn – crazy, crackpot, lunatic, eccentric, nut, weirdo, loony.

ant – sane, wise, sensible.

Kosher (adjective)

syn – admissible, allowable, permissible.

Kudos (noun)

syn – accolade, honor, laurel, distinction, applause, commendation, acclaim, eulogy, laudation, panegyric, plaudit, praise.

L

Label (noun)

syn – tag, categorise, pigeon-hole.

Labour (noun/verb)

syn – grind, toil, travail, work, drudgery, effort, strive, exertion, childbirth, delivery.

ant – idleness, rest, leisure.

Lacerate (verb)

syn – tear, sever, mangle, claw, tear, harrow, wound, rend, lancinate.

ant – mend, heal.

Lack (noun)

syn – absence, dearth, shortage, deficiency.

ant – abundance, sufficiency.

Lame (adjective)

syn – crippled, imperfect, weak, hamstrung, hobbled.

ant – strong, fit, healthy.

Lament (verb/noun)

syn – mourn, grieve, wail, moan, sorrow, dirge elegy, regret.

ant – rejoice, greet.

Languid (adjective)

syn – faint, dull, weak, feeble, torpid, listless, slow, sluggish, flagging, languishing

ant – flourishing, spirited, strong.

Lanky (adjective)

syn – angular, gangling, spindly, tall, rangy, raw-boned.

ant – fat, bukom, rounded.

Larceny (noun)

syn – theft, stealing, thievery, robbery, pilfering.

Large (adjective)

syn – big, huge, massive, giant, gigantic, mammoth, tremendous.

ant – small, tiny, puny.

Laugh (verb/noun)

syn – giggle, chortle, chuckle, guffaw, snicker, titter snigger.

ant – cry, weep.

Lawlessness (noun)

syn – anarchy, disorder, riot, disturbance.

ant – order, peace.

Lax (adjective)

syn – relaxed, lenient, loose, slack, soft, remiss, drooping.

ant – rigid, strict.

Laze (verb)

syn – loaf, loiter, lounge, idle, shirk, goof.

ant – industriousness.

Lead (noun/verb)

syn – conduct, direct, guide, leader, usher, pilot, precede, principal, protagonist, carry, extend, go, reach, run, stretch, escort, route, embark, commence, bring about, effectuate, pursue, initiate, preface, steer, undertake.

ant – follow.

League (noun)

syn – class, category, alliance, coalition, federation, union, confederacy.

ant – secession, disunion, separation.

Leap (noun/verb)

syn – bounce, bound, jump, spring, vault, hurdle, rise.

Learning (noun)

syn – erudition, knowledge, knowhow, pedantry.

ant – ignorance.

Lease (noun)

syn – charter, hire, let, rent.

ant – buy, purchase.

Leave (verb/noun)

syn – depart, go, retire, withdraw, abandon, desert, forsake.

ant – arrive, approach, stay.

Lenient (adjective)

syn – indulgent, lax, merciful, tolerant

ant – strict, rigid, stern.

Leery (adjective)

syn – distrustful, doubting, suspicious, mistrustful.

Legion (noun/adjective)

syn – army, crowd, drove, flock, mass, multitude, swarm, throng, group, myriad, numerous.

ant – solitary, only.

Leisure (noun)

syn – ease, repose, rest, relaxation.

ant – work, industry.

Lessen (verb)

syn – allay, assuage, alleviate, lighten, reduce, soften, temper, mitigate, palliatc, wane.

ant – escalate, increase.

Let (verb)

syn – lease, rent, permit, allow, approve, consent, endorse, permit, sanction, suffer, tolerate, emit, give, vent, absolve, spare, divulge, abate.

Level (noun/verb/adjective)

syn – degree, grade, point, stage, step, aim, cast, direct, head, demolish, destroy, raze, wreck, pulverize, flatten, equalize, smooth, straighten, even, flat.

ant – uneven.

Lewd (adjective)

syn – lascivious, obscene, wanton, lustful, prurient, salacious, lecherous, licentious.

ant – chaste, pure, moral, decorous.

Liaison (noun)

syn – connection, union, bond, relation, intrigue, illicit intimacy.

Liberal (adjective)

syn – generous, bountiful, tolerant, unbigoted, munificient, magnanimous, abundant, bounteous, plentiful, ample.

ant – rigid, stingy, scarce.

Licence (noun/verb)

syn – permission, permit, warrant, privilege, leave, liberty, certificate, dispensation, charter.

ant – prohibit, restrict.

Lick (noun/verb)

syn – bang, blow, clout, crack, hit, pound, sock,

swat, whack, wallop, attack, beat, flog, lash, thrash.

ant – soothe.

Lie (noun/verb)

syn – fib, falsehood, untruth, recline, rest, remain, extend, exist.

ant – truth, veracity.

Life (noun)

syn – being, body, creature, man, mortal, party, duration, existence, lifespan, animation, bounce, verve, zip, vigor, pep, sparkle, vivacity.

ant – death.

Lift (noun/verb)

syn - euphoria, boost, inspiration, elate, heave, hoist, disperse, dissipate, scatter, recall, rescind, repeal, upraise, arise, ascend, climb, mount, rise, pilfer, purloin, soar, heist, snitch, pinch.

ant – drop, sink.

Likely (adjective)

syn – possible, thinkable, presumable, hopeful, liable, prone, prospective, probable, apt, inclined, disposed.

ant – unlikely, impossible.

Limit (noun/verb)

syn – bound, confine, end, length, precinct, limitation, constraint, maximum, determine, confine, restrict, circumscribe.

ant – unlimited, unrestrained.

Limp (adjective/noun/verb)

syn – limber, flaccid, slack, relaxed, halt, hitch, hobble, lame gait.

ant – stiff, race.

Limpid (adjective)

syn – clear, lucid, pure, translucent, crystalline, transparent.

ant – opaque.

Lineage (noun)

syn – birth, blood, descent, family, line, origin, parentage, pedigree, seed, stock, clan, kindred, tribe.

Listen (verb)

syn – hear, attend, hearken, eavesdrop

ant – talk, ignore.

Listing (noun)

syn – catalogue, inventory, list, register, roll, roster.

Listless (adjective)

syn – languid, lethargic,

lackadaisical, languorous

ant – energetic, lively, spirited.

Literary (adjective)

syn – academic, pedantic, donnish, scholastic.

ant – illiterate, unlettered.

Liturgy (noun)

syn – observance, office, rite, ceremony, ritual, service.

Lively (adjective)

syn – brisk, spirited, vivacious, animated, buoyant

ant – listless, languid, dull.

Livid (adjective)

syn – pasty, sallow, waxen, pallid, colorless, ashen, bloodless.

Load (noun/verb)

syn – burden, cargo, goods, freight, responsibility

ant – unload.

Loathe (verb)

syn – abhor, hate, detest, despise, execrate, abominate.

ant – admire, idealise.

Lodgings (noun)

syn – accommodation, apartment, flat, quarters dwelling, hotel, motel, house.

Lofty (adjective)

syn – arrogant, insolent, lordly, haughty, overbearing, exalted, superior, proud, grand, august, elevated, towering.

Loneliness (noun)

syn – alienation, desolation, disaffection, estrangement.

ant – company, camaraderie.

Lonely (adjective)

syn – forlorn, remote, lonesome, solitary

ant – accompanied, escorted.

Look (verb/noun)

syn – gaze, glare, glance, peer, stare, vision.

ant – ignore.

Loom (verb)

syn – appear, emerge, issue, materialize, brew, impend, overhang, threaten.

Loophole (noun)

syn – opening loop, aperture, plea, pretext, excuse, pretence.

Loot (verb/noun)

syn – booty, haul, spoils,

swag, plunder, ransack.

Loquacious (adjective)

syn – talkative, blabbing, tattling, voluble, garrulous.

ant – reticent, taciturn.

Loss (noun)

syn – misplace, deprival, privation, dispossession, divestiture,

ant – gain, acquire.

Loud (adjective)

syn – blatant, noisy, obstreperous, vociferous, clamorous, boisterous.

ant – silent, subdued.

Lounge (verb)

syn – bum, idle, loaf, loiter, shirk.

ant – labor.

Lout (noun)

syn – gawk, hulk, oaf, ox, ungainly, dull-witted.

ant – sophisticated.

Love (verb/noun)

syn – crush, attachment, infatuation, affection, passion.

ant – dislike, hate.

Lucid (adjective)

syn – shining, clear, radiant, transparent, brilliant, distinct, diaphanous, sane, reasonable.

ant – opaque, dull, obscure.

Luck (noun)

syn – chance, fortuity, fortunateness.

ant – misfortune.

Lucre (noun)

syn – cash, currency, money.

Ludicrous (adjective)

syn – comic, comical, funny, farcical, ridiculous, risible, laughable.

ant – tragic, mournful.

Lugubrious (adjective)

syn – doleful, woebegone, sad, woeful, mournful, plaintive, rueful.

ant – happy, cheerful.

Luminous (adjective)

syn – gleaming, glistening, lambent, lucent, lucid, lustrous, refulgent.

ant – dull, gloomy, obscure.

Lurid (adjective)

syn – ghastly, grim, grisly, horrible, pale, pasty, wan, sallow, macabre, hideous.

ant – attractive, appealing.

Lurk (verb)

syn – creep, prowl, skulk, slink, sneak, steal.

ant – emerge.

Luscious (adjective)

syn - delicious, unctuous, palatable, savoury, delightful, pleasing.

ant – revolting, repugnant.

Lush (adjective)

syn- lavish, luxurious, plush, palatial, rich, opulent, extravagant.

ant – stark, austere.

Luxuriant (adjective)

syn – exuberant, profuse, plentiful, superabundant.

ant – sparse, scarce.

M

Machine (noun)

syn – apparatus, appliance, device, contrivance, engine, mechanism.

Mad (adjective)

syn – angry, indignant, ardent, keen, zealous, foolish, hare –brained, wild, frenzied, silly, zany, whacky, frantic, unsound, unbalanced, loony, insane, distraught, demented.

ant – genius, calm, intelligent.

Magnanimous (adjective)

syn – brave, noble, generous, dauntless, heroic, chivalrous, exalted, honourable.

ant – mean, selfish.

Magnetism (noun)

syn – allure, appeal, attraction, charisma, glamour, force, power.

ant – revulsion.

Magnitude (noun)

syn – size, greatness, grandeur, bulk, volume, extent, bigness, importance.

ant – insignificance.

Maintain (verb)

syn – sustain, hold, keep, support, preserve, uphold, upkeep, defend, continue, assert, declare, aver, contend, allege, vindicate, justify.

ant – attack, destroy.

Majestic (adjective)

syn – grandiose, noble,

splendid, princely, regal, imposing, superb, sublime, august, baronial.

ant – coarse, crude.

Make (verb)

syn – assemble, manufacture, produce, create, form, become, build.

ant – break, dismantle, destroy, undo.

Maladroit (adjective)

syn – awkward, inapt, inexpert, clumsy, unskilled, bungling.

ant – dexterous.

Malady (noun)

syn – disease, distemper, ailment, sickness, illness, indisposition, complaint, disorder.

ant – fitness, health.

Malediction (noun)

syn – anathema, curse, damnation, execration.

ant – blessing.

Malign (adjective/verb)

syn – asperse, defame, libel, slander, vilify, revile, malicious, malevolent, pernicious, abuse, defame, disparage, traduce.

ant – praise, commend.

Manacle (noun/verb)

syn – bond, chain, handcuff, restraint, shackle, leash, tie, trammel.

ant – release, liberate.

Manifest (adjective/verb)

syn – apparent, obvious, plain, evident, clear, visible, glaring, distinct, conspicuous, show, exhibit, reveal, disclose, display, evince, expose, express.

ant – conceal, camouflage.

Manipulate (verb)

syn – handle, exploit, play, manoeuvre, ply, wield.

Mankind (noun)

syn – humanity, homosapiens, man, men.

Mannerism (noun)

syn – airs, affectation, exhibitionism, preciosity, pose, characteristic, temperament.

Manufacture (verb)

syn – assemble, build, fabricate, frame, mould, produce, shape, put together, forge, construct.

ant – destroy.

Marginal (adjective)

syn – inconsequential, minor, negligible, nugatory, peripheral, piddling.

ant – central, significant.

Marsh (noun)

syn – swamp, paddy, fen, morass, everglade, bog.

Marvellous (adjective)

syn – amazing, fantastic, incredible, fabulous, wonderful, terrific, great, unbelievable, splendid.

ant – terrible.

Masculine (adjective)

syn – male, manly, virile, husky.

ant – feminine

Masquerade (noun)

syn – mask, revel, disguise, veil, cover.

Massive (adjective)

syn – enormous, huge, hefty, immense, vast, ponderous.

ant – minute, small.

Mastermind (noun/verb)

syn – paragon, principal, chief, master-spirit.

Mature (adjective/verb)

syn – aged, experienced, develop, mellow, ripen, full-grown, adult.

ant – regress, childish.

Maudlin (adjective)

syn – mawkish, sentimental, soft, slushy, mushy, drippy, tear-jerking, romantic.

ant – practical, rational.

Meagre (adjective)

syn – thin, lean, gaunt, emaciated, feeble, vapid, barren, dull, prosy, small, scanty.

ant – ample, fat, rich.

Mean (adjective/verb/noun)

syn – connote, denote, imply, indicate, signify, hint, suggest, symbolize, meaning, selfish, self-centred, stingy, miserly, average.

ant – generous, honorable, extreme.

Meander (verb/noun)

syn – labyrinth, winding, maze, serpentine, turn, flowing course, wander.

Meddlesome (adjective)

syn – nosy, interfering, intrusive, prying, snoopy, officious, obtrusive.

ant – unobtrusive, distant.

Mediate (adjective/verb)

syn – intercede, interpose, intervene, arbitrate.

ant – incite, indifferent.

Mediocre (adjective)

syn – commonplace, ordinary, mean, average, fair, passable, tolerable, medium.

ant – outstanding, excellent, superior.

Medley (noun)

syn – mixture, jumble, miscellany, mish-mash, potpouri, farrago.

Meet (verb/adjective)

syn – contact, encounter, see all, receive, match.

ant – avoid.

Meeting (noun)

syn – assemblage, assembly, conclave, conference, congregation, congress, convention, council, convocation, gathering.

Melancholic (adjective)

syn – dejected, depressed, sombre, gloomy, dismal, unhappy, mournful, dispirited.

ant – jocose, jocund, merry.

Mellifluence (noun)

syn – smoothness, softness, sweetness, mellowness, soft flow.

ant – harsh, jarring.

Melody (noun)

syn – air, aria, dell, song, theme, tune.

ant – discord, tuneless.

Melt (verb)

syn – dissolve, thaw, liquefy, soften, disappear.

ant – freeze, solidify.

Mendacity (noun)

syn – habitual lying, duplicity, deceit, falsehood, untruthfulness, deception.

ant – sincerity, honesty.

Mentor (noun/verb)

syn – adviser, counsellor, consultant, guide, recommend.

ant – adversary.

Mercurial (adjective)

syn – lively, nimble, active, spirited, jay, flighty, inconstant, volatile, fickle, mobile.

ant – constant, steadfast.

Merit (noun)

syn – excellence, value, worth, virtue.

ant – flaw, worthlessness.

Merge (verb)

syn – immerse, submerge, sink, bury, lose, be swallowed, involve.

ant – dissociate, separate.

Method (noun)

syn – fashion, manner, mode, system, procedure, way.

Migrate (verb)

syn – emigrate, move, travel, journey, immigrate

ant – remain.

Mind (noun/verb)

syn – brains, head, intellect, intelligence, reason, wits, object, troubled by, upset.

ant – ignore, neglect.

Minister (noun/verb)

syn – brother, monk, pastor, preacher, priest, reverend, care, attend, look after.

Minute (adjective)

syn – infinitesimal, microscopic, miniature, minuscule.

ant – large, massive.

Miscellaneous (adjective)

syn – various, mixed, diversified, mingled, heterogeneous.

ant – specific, particular.

Mischievous (adjective)

syn – naughty, prankster, playful, teasing

ant – sombre, serious.

Misdemeanor (noun)

syn – fault, transgression, trespass, misdeed, misconduct, misbehavior, offence.

ant – decorous.

Misery (noun)

syn – agony, anguish, discomfort, distress, passion, torment, torture, harm, hurt, pain.

ant – happiness, pleasure.

Mislay (verb)

syn – lose, misplace, find, astray.

ant – find, recover.

Misleading (adjective)

syn – deceitful, deceptive, delusive, trick, falsehood, guile, dissembling.

ant – honest, genuine, sincre.

Mistake (noun/verb)

syn – blunder, boner, error, goof, slip, faux pas, contretemps, flaw.

ant – correct, rectify.

Mitigate (verb)

syn – moderate, appease, soothe, soften, pacify, quell, allay, temper, alleviate, abate, lessen, diminish, assuage.

ant – aggravate, exaggerate.

Mixture (noun)

syn – alloy, blend, amalgam, composite, compound, combination.

ant – separate

Moderate (adjective/verb)

syn – mediocre, temperature, frugal, sparing, limited, judicious, mild, gentle, repress, subdue, blent, dull, pacify, mitigate, temper, control.

ant – extreme, aggravate.

Modest (adjective)

syn – humble, lowly, meek, shy, retiring, timid, unassuming, unpretentious.

ant – conceited, arrogant, pretentious, immodest.

Momentous (adjective)

syn – important, significant, grave, serious, weighty.

ant – trivial, insignificant.

Monotonous (adjective)

syn – boring, dull, tedious, tiresome.

ant – exciting, varied.

Moody (adjective)

syn – angry, irritable, capricious, variable, sullen, ill-tempered, morose, pensive, peevish, fretful, glum, intractable, snappy, irascible.

ant – equable, affable, amiable.

Moral (noun/adjective)

syn – decent, ethical, good, honorable, upright, virtuous, righteous, psychological.

ant – genius, intellectual.

Mordacious (adjective)

syn – acerbic, acid, acrid, astringent, biting, caustic, pungent, scathing, stinging, truculent, vitriolic, corrosive, mordant.

ant – mellow, complimentary.

Moron (noun)

syn – dull, dimwit, idiot, clot, imbecible, simpleton, twerp, numbskull.

ant – immoral, unethical,

dishonourable.

Mother (noun)

syn – ancestor, forbear, parent, progenitor, beginning, origin, provenance, root, spring.

Mottled (adjective)

syn – spotted, motley, speckled, variegated, piebald.

ant – smooth, plain.

Mould (noun/verb)

syn – model, fashion, forge, form, sculpt, shape.

Mountain (noun)

syn – ciff, hill, hillock, plateau, precipice, range, tableland, promontory.

ant – plains, valley.

Muffle (verb)

syn – wrap, cover, shroud, envelop, conceal, disguise.

ant – expose.

Munificent (adjective)

syn – liberal, generous, bounteous, princely, free.

ant – mean, selfish, stingy.

Muse (noun/verb)

syn – reverie, musing, abstraction, ponder, reflect, think, ruminate, brood, consider.

Mutual (adjective)

syn – common, joint, reciprocal, shared, interchangeable.

ant – separate, individual.

Myopic (adjective)

syn – near-sighted, dim-sighted, short-sighted.

ant – far-sighted, long-sighted.

Mystical (adjective)

syn – mysterious, occult, supernatural, bizarre.

ant – logical.

Myth (noun)

syn – legend, fable, lore, tradition, figment, fantasy, fiction.

ant – truth, reality.

N

Nab (verb)

syn – apprehend, arrest, seize, bust, catch, run in, grab.

ant – release, free, liberate.

Nag (verb)

syn – carp, fuss, peck at, pick on.

ant – praise, applaud, commend.

Nail (verb)

syn – capture, catch, net, get, secure, take.

ant – free, release.

Naive (adjective)

syn – artless, guileless, rude, unaffected, provincial, ingenuous, unsophisticated.

ant – formal, sophisticated.

Namby-pamby (adjective)

syn – bland, insipid, vapid, jejune, wishy-washy.

Name (noun/verb)

syn – call, christen, designate, dub, appoint, choose, label, reputation.

Nap (noun/verb)

syn – catnap, doze, siesta, snooze.

ant – awake, conscious.

Narcissism (noun)

syn – egoism, pride, conceit, self-love, vanity.

ant – altruism.

Narcotic (noun/adjective)

syn – drug, opiate, hypnotic, soporific, sedative.

Narrative (noun)

syn – anecdote, legend, myth, saga, story, tale, yarn, history, news, report.

Narrow (verb/adjective)

syn – constrict, constringe, insular, limited, local, parochial, provincial, petty, narrow-minded, close, confining, cramped, crowded, snug, tight.

ant – broad, wide.

Nascence (noun)

syn – beginning, birth, outset, commencement, genesis, dawn, onset, inception.

ant – closure, finale.

Nastiness (noun)

syn – ill will, malice, malevolence, spite, venom, viciousness.

ant – pleasing, charming.

Nasty (adjective)

syn – filthy, foul, squalid, abominable, abhorrent, rotten, shabby, vile, infamous, odious, obnoxious, repugnant, bad-tempered, snappy, evil, hateful, venomous, gross, lewd, vicious, malignant, profane, ugly, revolting.

ant – nice, cheerful, welcoming.

Native (adjective/verb)

syn – aboriginal, endemic, indigenous, natural, inborn.

ant – alien, foreign, immigrant.

National (noun/adjective)

syn – citizen, subject, domestic, home, internal, native, civil, civic.

ant – foreign, alien.

Natural (adjective)

syn – innocent, naïve, artless, unaffected, guileless, inborn, inbred, casual, easygoing, native, relaxed, spontaneous, real, sincere, true.

ant – unnatural, spurious.

Nature (noun)

syn – character, makeup, disposition, temper, temperament, complexion, personality.

Naughty (adjective)

syn – improper, mischievous, impish, unseemly, indecorous.

ant – staid, decorous.

Nausea (noun)

syn – qualm, squeamishness, loathing, seasickness, disgust, aversion, repugnance.

Nautical (adjective)

syn – marine, maritime, navigational.

Near (verb/adjective/adverb)

syn – approach, adjacent, immediate, nearby, contiguous, close.

ant – far, distant.

Nearby (adjective/adverb)

syn – adjacent, close, near, nigh, immediate, accessible, convenient, handy, proximate.

ant – far, distant, remote.

Neat (adjective)

syn – fabulous, tidy, clean, organised, orderly, spruced up, clean, deft, plain, unblended, undiluted, unmixed.

ant – dirty, disorganised.

Nebulous (adjective)

syn – ambiguous, cloudy, inexplicit, vague, obscure, unclear, uncertain, equivocal.

ant – definite, explicit.

Necessity (noun)

syn – call, cause, ground, occasion, reason, why, wherefore, condition, must, need, requirement, exigency.

ant – luxury, optional.

Neck and neck (adjective)

syn – close, nip and tuck, tight, near.

Necessary (adjective)

syn – essential, needful, indispensable, required, compulsory, imperative, mandatory, requisite.

ant – optional.

Need (noun/verb)

syn – must, necessity, precondition, demand, charge, duty, obligation,penury, privation, want, lack, require.

Needy (adjective)

syn – beggarly, poor, impoverished, destitute, penniless, penurious, impecunious, broke.

ant – rich, wealthy, well off.

Negate (verb)

syn – abolish, annul, abrogate, invalidate, nullify, cancel, neutralize, deny, contradict, contravene.

ant – affirm, confirm.

Negligent (adjective)

syn – derelict, lax, neglectful, remiss, slack.

ant – careful, cautious.

Negotiate (verb)

syn – arrange, conclude, fix, set, settle, haggle, palter, bargain.

Neglect (verb)

syn – ignore, disregard, dereliction, thoughtlessness.

ant – attention, consideration.

Nerd (noun)

syn – jerk, fool, idiot, moron, nincompoop, simpleton, imbecile, cretin.

ant – sane, genius, intellectual.

Neighbouring (verb)

syn – abutting, adjacent, adjoining, juxtaposed, contiguous, semi-detached.

ant – dispersed, scattered.

Nefarious (adjective)

syn – abominable, detestable, wicked, infamous, heinous, wicked, vile, dreadful, execrable.

ant – commendable, exemplary.

Nervous (adjective)

syn – edgy, excitable, fidgety, flighty, jumpy, jittery, restless, uptight, uneasy.

ant – calm, equable, composed.

Nest egg (noun)

syn – store, treasure, cache, hoard, inventory, reserve, reservoir, stock, stash.

Nestle (verb)

syn – cuddle, nuzzle, snug, snuggle.

Net (noun, verb)

syn – mesh, netting, network, web, capture, catch, get, secure, take, bring in, draw, earn, gain, gross, pay, produce, realize, repay, return, yield.

Nethermost (adjective)

syn – lowest, bottom, lowermost, nadir.

ant – peak, summit, pinnacle.

Nettle (verb)

syn – aggravate, provoke, gall, annoy, bother, bug, chafe, fret, exasperate, irritate, peeve, rile, ruffle, vex.

ant – please, charm.

Neutralise (verb)

syn – counterbalance, offset, invalidate, cancel, minimise.

ant – intensify, magnify.

New (adjective)

syn – fresh, additional, original, novel, innovative, current, contemporary.

ant – old, dated.

Newcomer (noun)

syn – alien, foreign, outsider, stranger.

ant – native.

Nexus (noun)

syn – bond, knot, ligament, ligature, link, tie, yoke, connect.

Nicety (noun)

syn – accuracy, exactness, precision, truth, refinement, elegance.

ant – inaccuracy, coarseness.

Nictate (verb)

syn – bat, blink, twinkle, wink.

Nifty (adjective)

syn – superb, splendid, terrific, wonderful, great, fantastic, tremendous.

ant – dowdy, grungy.

Niggardly (adjective)

syn – parsimonious, stingy, avaricious, miserly, sordid, mean, tight-fisted, chary.

ant – generous.

Nigh (adjective, adverb)

syn – adjacent, close, contiguous, immediate, near, nearby, proximate.

ant – distant, far, remote.

Nihility (noun)

syn – nonexistent, nothing, nothingness, absence.

ant – presence.

Nimble (adjective)

syn – adroit, clever, deft, dexterous, facile, handy, spry, agile, quick, brisk.

ant – slow, clumsy.

Nip (verb/noun)

syn – blast, blight, dash, bolt, dart, flash, flit, race, rocket, whirl, whisk, zip, zoom, drink, shot, sip, tot.

Nitwit (noun)

syn – ass, fool, idiot, imbecile, moron, ninny, simpleton, jerk, nerd.

ant – sensible, wise, clever.

Nix (noun/verb/adverb)

syn – nil, nothing, null, refuse, reject, spurn, turn down, veto, nay.

ant – accept, endorse.

Nobility (noun)

syn – blue blooded, noblesse, gentry, aristocracy, society, upper class, upper crust, who's who, elite.

ant – riff-raff, tramp, bourgeois.

Noble (adjective)

syn – elevated, moral, imposing, lordly, magnificent, august, baronial, regal, princely, sublime, thoroughbred, majestic.

ant – ignoble, trashy, menial, plebian.

Nobody (noun/pronoun)

syn – cipher, nonentity, nothing, zero, none, no one.

Nod (noun/verb)

syn – acceptance, consent, yes, accept, kowtow, acquiesce, agree, assent, catnap, snooze, siesta.

ant – shake, dissent.

Noise (noun)

syn – blare, sound, clatter, din, racket, uproar, hubbub.

ant – quiet, silence.

Nomadic (adjective)

syn – vagabond, vagrant, peripatetic.

Nonaligned (adjective)

syn – impartial, neuter, neutral, unbiased, uninvolved, unprejudiced, fair.

ant – aligned, biased.

Nonappearance (noun)

syn – absence, nonattendance.

ant – present, attending.

Nonchalant (adjective)

syn – calm, collected, poised, even, detached, unflappable, possessed, cool, composed, unruffled.

ant – nervous, agitated.

Noncommittal (adjective)

syn – controlled, inhibited, reserved, restrained, impassive.

ant – expressive.

Nonconformist (noun)

syn – dissenter, dissident,

heretic, radical, schismatic, sectarian, separatist.

ant – conservative, conformist.

Nonentity (noun)

syn – cipher, nobody, nothing.

ant – VIP, celebrity, famous.

Nonplus (verb/noun)

syn – puzzle, confound, confuse, perplexity, poser, disconcert, quandary.

ant – clarify, enlighten.

Norm (noun)

syn – average, mean, median, medium, par, commonplace, ordinary, rule, usual.

ant – exception.

Normal (adjective)

syn – natural, ordinary, regular, typical, general.

ant – abnormal, atypical, queer.

Nostrum (noun)

syn – cure, elixir, medication, medicine, remedy.

ant – ailment, sickness.

Nosy (adjective)

syn – curious, inquisitive, snoopy.

ant – detached.

Notable (noun/adjective)

syn – name, personage, character, dignitary, leader, eminence, famous, great, illustrious, noted, renowned.

ant – infamous.

Note (noun/verb)

syn – comment, obiter dictum, observation, remark, annotation, commentary, distinction, fame, glory, eminence, prestige, melody, tune, badge, evidence, index, indication, mark, heed, notice, remark, descry, detect, discern.

ant – ignore, overlook.

Noticeable (adjective)

syn – apparent, obvious, manifest, distinct, marked, salient, perceptible, evident, arresting, conspicuous.

ant – ambiguous, vague.

Notion (noun)

syn – concept, idea, sentiment, opinion, belief, view, estimation, conviction, expectation.

Nourish (verb)

syn – bear, harbour, nurse,

feed, foster, nurture, cultivate.

ant – destroy.

Novel (adjective/noun)

syn – new, strange, unusual, fresh, rare, tale, romance, story, fiction.

ant – non-fiction, reality.

Noxious (adjective)

syn – baneful, toxic, deadly, pestilent, virulent, malignant, pernicious.

ant – remedial, medicinal.

Nucleus (noun)

syn – bud, embryo, germ, kernel, seed, spark.

Nudge (noun/verb)

syn – dig, jab, jog, poke, prod.

Nugget (noun)

syn – chunk, clod, clump, lump.

Nuisance (noun)

syn – aggravation, annoyance, peeve, irritation, plague, torment, vexation, bother.

Nullify (verb)

syn – abolish, veto, abrogate, annul, negate, vitiate, void, cancel, neutralize.

ant – accept, endorse.

Numb (adjective)

syn – anaesthetised, deadened, insensible, paralysed, stupefied, listless, sloth, impassive.

ant – sensitive, aware.

Nurse (verb)

syn – bear, harbour, nourish, foster, cultivate, nurture.

Nurture (noun/verb)

syn – nourishment, feed, nurse, tend, instruct, breed, care, attention, diet.

ant – destroy.

Nuzzle (verb)

syn – cuddle, snug, snuggle, nestle.

ant – repel.

O

Oath (noun)

syn – pledge, vow, promise, curse, expletive, malediction.

Obedient (adjective)

syn – dutiful, good, well-behaved, compliant.

ant – obdurate, disobedient.

Obligation (noun)

syn – duty, function, office, responsibility.

ant – right.

Obliterate (verb)

syn – efface, erase, expunge, cancel, wipe, destroy, rub, blot out.

ant – restore, build.

Oblivious (adjective)

syn – forgetful, absent-minded, abstracted, inattentive, heedless, negligent.

ant – aware, observant.

Obnoxious (adjective)

syn – hateful, odious, offensive.

ant – pleasing, lovable.

Obscure (adjective)

syn – dim, abstruse, arcane, cryptic, vague, remote, sombre, dark, gloomy, indefinite, indistinct, retired, secluded, shadowy, murky.

ant – clear, explicit, definitive.

Obsequious (adjective)

syn – sycohantic, fawning, flattering, servile, subservient,meanly, submissive.

ant – contumelious, overbearing

Observant (adjective)

syn – alert, attentive, aware,

discerning, perceptive.

ant – oblivious, preoccupied.

Obsessed (verb)

syn – addicted, addictive, compulsive, hooked.

ant – spontaneous, natural.

Obsolete (adjective)

syn – antiquated, obsolescent, discussed, neglected, ancient, archaic, past, outdated.

ant – modern, contemporary.

Obstacle (noun)

syn – bar, barricade, barrier, difficulty, hurdle, impediment, snag.

ant – assistance, aid.

Obtuse (adjective)

syn – blunt, dull, stupid, stolid, stockish, heavy, slow, dim-witted.

ant – intellectual, smart, pointed.

Obvious (adjective)

syn – exposed, liable, subject, plain, evident, patent, manifest, palpable, distinct, overt.

ant – hidden, concealed, latent, covert.

Occasional (adjective)

syn – casual, desultory, fitful, infrequent, intermittent, rare, periodic, sporadic.

ant – regular, frequent.

Offer (noun/verb)

syn – bid, present, proffer, propose, tender, volunteer.

ant – reject, withold.

Offhand (adjective/ adverb)

syn – extempore, impromptu, unstudied, readily, unrehearsed, unpremeditated, spontaneous.

ant – prepared, rehearsed, premeditated.

Officious (adjective)

syn – meddlesome, interfering, obtrusive, busy, pushing, arrogant.

ant – aloof, distant.

Old (adjective/noun)

syn – aged, elderly, senile, venerable, patriarchal, former, familiar, worn-out.

ant – new, young.

Old-fashioned (adjective/noun)

syn – archaic, antiquated, antediluvan, obsolete, out of date, passe, ancient.

ant – modern, up-to-date.

Omen (noun)

syn – prognastic, presage, augury, sign, auspice, portent.

Omniscient (adjective)

syn – wise, all-knowing, all-seeing.

ant – ignorant.

Onerous (adjective)

syn – burden, heavy, weighty, hard, difficult, oppressive.

ant – light.

Opaque (adjective)

syn – obscure, clouded, turbid, non-transparent.

ant – lucid, transparent.

Opinion (noun)

syn – belief, estimate, conviction, impression, view, sentiment.

ant – fact.

Opponent (noun)

syn – adversary, foe, rival, enemy, antagonist, competitor.

ant – associate, ally.

Opportune (adjective)

syn – advantageous, politic, expedient, convenient, seasonable, timely, fortunate, lucky, fit.

ant – inopportune, untimely.

Opportunistic (adjective)

syn – aspiring, pushy, ambitious.

ant – indolent, lazy.

Opposed (verb)

syn – adverse, antagonistic, inimical, against.

ant – complementary, compatible.

Optimistic (adjective)

syn – confident, hopeful, sanguine, positive.

ant – pessimistic, defeatist.

Opulence (noun)

syn – wealth, riches, fortune, affluence, money.

ant – penury, pecuniary.

Orderly (adjective)

syn – natty, neat, tidy, trim, organised, clean.

ant – disorganised, chaotic.

Organize (verb)

syn – arrange, classify, marshal, order, sort.

ant – disorganize, bungle, mess.

Ornament (noun)

syn – adorn, garnish, decorate, embellish, deck, beautify.

ant –disfigure, mar.

Ostentatious (adjective)

syn – vain, boastful, dashing, flaunting, pompous, pretentious, show, gaudy.

ant – reserved, modest.

Outrage (noun/verb)

syn – aggravate, bug, exasperate, insult, affront, indignity, abuse, maltreat, offend.

ant – favour, soothe.

Outrageous (adjective)

syn – atrocious, monstrous, shocking, scandalous, unspeakable.

ant – decorous, commendable.

Outspoken (adjective)

syn – plain, blunt, frank, candid, forthright, straightforward.

ant – taciturn, subtle.

Outstanding (adjective)

syn – distinguished, dominant, foremost, paramount, predominant, prevailing, prominent.

ant – mediocre.

Overbearing (adjective)

syn – arrogant, haughty, imperious, domineering.

ant – docile, deferential.

Overhear (verb)

syn – bug, eavesdrop, snoop, monitor, wiretap.

Overlook (verb)

syn – view, inspect, superintend, supervise, disregard, slight, oversee, excuse, forgive, pardon.

ant – observe, note.

Overwhelm (verb)

syn – overflow, overpower, overcome, subdue, conquer, defeat, swamp, drown.

ant – submit.

P

Pacify (verb)

syn – assuage, calm, quiet, lull, smooth, appease, tranquilise, quell, allay, soften, mollify.

ant – aggravate, excite.

Pain (noun)

syn – ache, pang, stitch, throe, twinge, harm, hurt.

ant – pleasure.

Palatable (adjective)

syn – agreeable, enjoyable, toothsome, delicious, nice, appetizing, tasteful, luscious.

ant – bland, unappetizing.

Pale (adjective/noun)

syn – ashen, pallid, wan, livid, cadaverous.

ant – colourful, flushed, ruddy.

Palpitate (verb)

syn – pulsate, throb, tremble, quiver, shiver.

Paltry (adjective)

syn – base, small, little, insignificant, unimportant, trifling, trivial, pitiful, contemptible, low, shabby, shuffling, abject, wretched.

ant – considerable.

Pamper (verb)

syn – baby, coddle, humour, indulge, mollycoddle, spoil.

ant – ignore, neglect, discipline.

Parasite (noun)

syn – bludger, cadger, freeloader, hanger-on, leech, sponger.

ant – host.

Paraphernalia (noun)

syn – appendage, ornament, accoutrement, equipage, trapping, appurtenance.

Pardon (verb)

syn – condone, excuse, forgive, overlook, remit.

ant – convict, punish.

Parity (noun)

syn – equality, likeness, equivalence, sameness, analogy.

ant – disparity.

Parochial (adjective)

syn – parish, petty, narrow, provincial.

ant – broad-minded.

Part (noun/verb)

syn – passage, piece, portion, section, segment, subdivision, separate, dissociate, role in play.

ant – whole, totality, meet.

Passionate (adjective)

syn – ardent, burning, fervent, fury, fervid, vehement, zealous.

ant – indifferent, impassive, apathetic.

Passing (adjective/adverb/preposition)

syn – transient, surpassing, exceeding, excessively, fleeting, momentary, beyond, over.

ant – stationary, permanent.

Pathetic (adjective)

syn – pitiable, moving, poignant, touching, pitiful.

ant – farcical, ridiculous.

Patience (noun)

syn – forbearance, stoicism, sufferance, resignation, perseverance, endurance.

ant – impatince.

Pathos (noun)

syn – passion, tenderness, emotion, poignance, pity.

ant – joyous, merry.

Paucity (noun)

syn – few, small, rarity, scarcity.

ant – abundance, prosperity.

Peccadillo (noun)

syn – fault, slight, offence, trespass, blunder, escapade.

ant – decorous.

Peculiar (adjective)

syn – typical, individual, characteristic, select, particular, specific.

ant – general.

Pedestrian (noun/ adjective)

syn – traveller, walker, hiker, dull, uninteresting.

ant – passenger, interesting.

Pedigree (noun)

syn – lineage, descent, ancestry, line, extraction, genealogy, stock.

Penalty (noun)

syn – punishment, handicap, fine, mulct, retribution, forfeiture.

ant – pardon.

Penchant (noun)

syn – inclination, bent, propensity, proclivity, turn, leaning, liking, bias, predilection.

ant – aversion, dislike.

Pending (adjective/ preposition)

syn – due, depending, undetermined, during.

ant – settled.

Penniless (verb)

syn – destitute, needy, indigent, necessitous, penurious.

ant – affluent, wealthy.

People (noun)

syn – herd, mob, populace, rabble, masses, folk, kin.

ant – elite, aristocracy.

Perception (noun)

syn – seeing, vision, sensation, recognition, cognition, perceptivity, discernment, understanding.

ant – ignorance, blindness.

Perdition (noun)

syn – ruin, destruction, wreck, downfall, loss, misery, demolition.

ant – prosperity, growth.

Peregrination (noun)

syn – travel, wandering, journey, tour, voyage.

Perennial (adjective)

syn – lasting, enduring, permanent, undying, ceaseless, perpetual, immortal, continual, constant, unceasing.

ant – temporary, seasonal, transient.

Perfect (adjective/verb)

syn – consummate, flawless, ideal.

ant – imperfect, flawed.

Perforate (verb)

syn – pierce, penetrate, punch, prick, bore, riddle, drill, puncture.

ant – mend, plug.

Perfunctory (adjective)

syn – indifferent, careless, mechanical, routine, formal, unmindful, slovenly, slight.

ant – thorough, detailed.

Perilous (adjective)

syn – dangerous, hazardous, risky.

ant – safe, secure.

Period (noun)

syn – aeon, age, cycle, era, epoch, generation.

Periphery (noun)

syn – outside, perimeter, boundary, circumference, girth.

ant – centre, nucleus.

Permanent (adjective)

syn – abiding, durable, enduring, indelible, lasting, perennial, perpetual, stable.

ant – temporary, transient.

Permeate (verb)

syn – imbue, impregnate, penetrate, saturate, pervade, pass through.

ant – block, hinder.

Perplex (verb)

syn – confuse, confound, mystify, complicate, snarl, bewilder, nonplus, fog, worry, annoy, pester, bother.

ant – clarify, enlighten, simplify.

Persevere (verb)

syn – persist, steady, constant, steadfast, firm, patient, dogged.

ant – waver, vary.

Persistent (adjective)

syn – constant, obstinate, pertinacious, obdurate, fixed, tenacious, steady, enduring, lasting, unremitting, ceaseless, incessant, continual.

ant – periodic, occasional.

Perspicacious (adjective)

syn – acute, discerning, shrewd, sagacious, keen, sharp-sighted, perceptive, penetrating.

ant – obtuse, ignorant.

Persuade (verb)

syn – advise, counsel, convince, impel, influence, incite, lead, entice, allure, prevail.

ant – deter.

Pert (adjective)

syn – lively, saucy, cheeky, impudent, flippant, dapper, nimble, perky, sprightly.

ant – bashful, coy.

Petrify (verb)

syn – scare, amaze, dumbfound, paralyse, astound, benumb, deaden.

ant – reassure.

Physical (adjective)

syn – bodily, carnal, corporeal, fleshy, material, mesomorphic.

ant – mental, moral.

Pierce (verb)

syn – penetrate, prick, stab, probe, permeate.

ant – mend, heal.

Pig (noun)

syn – boar, hog, porker, sow, swine.

Pinnacle (noun)

syn – top, summit, apex, acme, peak, turret, minaret, zenith.

ant – base, nadir.

Piquant (noun)

syn – stinging, biting, pungent, sparkling, sharp, severe, cutting, offensive, vexatious.

ant – dull, bland.

Placid (adjective)

syn – serene, cool, collected, composed, equable, unruffled, tranquil, peaceful, quiet.

ant – excited, agitated.

Plain (adjective/noun)

syn – bush, desert, pampas, tundra, range, apparent, evident, manifest, obvious, conspicuous, frank, candid, simple, unostentatious, uncomplicated.

ant – fancy, obscure, uneven, devious.

Plan (noun/verb)

syn – blueprint, design, proposal, programme, scheme, action, method, drawing, diagram.

Playful (adjective)

syn – frisky, frolicsome, sportive, light-hearted,

merry, jovial.

ant – listless, sedate.

Plead (verb)

syn – appeal, beseech, request, beg, entreat, implore, pray, supplicate.

ant – command, order, demand.

Pleasing (adjective)

syn – agreeable, attractive, engaging, nice, pleasant, gratifying, enjoyable, charming.

ant – displeasing, obnoxious, repulsive.

Pleasure (noun)

syn – delight, ecstasy, enjoyment, fun, glee, joy, rapture, happiness, delectation.

ant – displeasure, misery.

Pledge (noun)

syn – bail, bond, collateral, guarantee, security, recognizance, surety, vow, promise.

Plethora (noun)

syn – plentitude, abundance, excess, surfeit, superfluity, redundancy, repletion.

ant – scarcity.

Pliable (adjective)

syn – flexible, pliant, supple, lithe, yielding, manageable, adaptable, compliant.

ant – rigid, stiff, intractable.

Plunder (verb/noun)

syn – ravage, sack, loot, pillage, ransack.

ant – restore.

Ponderous (adjective)

syn – heavy, weighty, bulky, laboured, important, mighty, forcible.

ant – dainty, light.

Poor (adjective)

syn – hard-up, underprivileged, penurious.

ant – rich, wealthy, affluent.

Portray (verb)

syn – depict, describe, represent, sketch, delineate.

Portend (verb)

syn – predict, presage, augur, forebode, indicate, signify, prognosticate, foreshadow.

Portly (noun)

syn – stately, grand, majestic, stout, plump, fleshy, magisterial, dignified, imposing, bulky, corpulent.

ant – lean, lanky, emaciated.

Poser (noun)

syn – riddle, enigma, puzzle, mystery, knotty problem.

ant – answer.

Possess (verb)

syn – hold, keep, control, dominate, have, own.

ant – borrow, relinquish, dispossess.

Posterity (noun)

syn – descendant, progeny, offspring, children, heir.

ant – ancestry.

Postpone (verb)

syn – defer, delay, adjourn, retard, suspend, procrastinate, shelve.

ant – schedule.

Potent (adjective)

syn – strong, forcible, powerful, cogent, influential, intense, mighty, able, capable.

ant – impotent, weak.

Practical (adjective)

syn – proficient, trained, skilled, workable, useful, effective.

ant – theoretical.

Praise (verb)

syn – eulogise, acclaim, commend, extol, land, applaud, encomium.

ant – censure, criticism.

Precinct (noun)

syn – limit, boundary, confine, border, frontier, neighbourhood, terminus, district, area.

Precipitate (verb/adjective)

syn – throw, hurl, fling, hasten, hurry, speed, forward, expedite, urge, despatch, hasty, impetuous, violent, abrupt, sudden.

ant – retard, cautious.

Precursor (noun)

syn – forerunner, harbinger, herald, pioneer, omen, sign, prognostic, inkling.

ant – follower.

Predatory (adjective)

syn – plundering, ravaging, ravenous, pillaging, greedy, aggressive.

ant – submissive.

Predicament (noun)

syn – situation, condition, state, position, dilemma, quandary, corner, scrape, fix, impasse.

Prejudiced (adjective)

syn – biased, bigoted, partial, unfair, partisan.

ant – impartial, fair.

Premature (adjective)

syn – early, untimely, hasty, precipitate, unripe, unprepared.

ant – mature, seasoned, veteran.

Preoccupied (verb)

syn – absorbed, engrossed, involved.

ant – distracted, attentive.

Present (adjective/noun/verb)

syn – bonus, gift, grant, gratuity, largess, tip, show, occurring, being, give, award.

ant – past.

Presume (verb)

syn – suppose, opinion, assume, think, conjecture, surmise, believe, infer, deduce, venture, consider, presuppose.

ant – knowledge, factual.

Prevalent (adjective)

syn – widespread, abundant, ample, common, copious, plentiful, prevailing, rife.

ant – occasional, scanty.

Prevaricate (verb)

syn – deviate, shift, dodge, evade truth, palter, cavil, shuffle, equivocate.

ant – honesty, veracity.

Prevent (verb)

syn – avert, forestall, obviate, preclude, stop, avoid, thwart, hinder.

ant – aid, encourage.

Privacy (noun)

syn – isolation, seclusion, solitude, withdrawal.

ant – company, publicity.

Probe (verb)

syn – prove, test, verify, investigate, sift, explore, look, scrutinize, sound, fathom.

ant – ignore, neglect.

Procrastinate (verb)

syn – dally, postpone, stall, dawdle, lag, loiter, tarry, dilly-dally.

ant – action, expedite.

Proclivity (noun)

syn – inclination, tendency, aptitude, propensity, bias, disposition, learning, bent, predisposition, drift, direction.

ant – aversion.

Profanity (noun)

syn – irreverence, blasphemy, profaneness, swearing, cursing, obscenity, vulgarity.

ant – reverence.

Profession (noun)

syn – field, job, occupation, trade, work, vocation.

Profound (adjective)

syn – deep, abysmal, heavy, penetrating, skilled, sagacious, fathomless.

ant – shallow, superficial.

Prohibit (verb)

syn – hinder, prevent, forbid, inhibit, disallow, preclude, debar.

ant – permit, aid.

Prolong (verb)

syn – lengthen, sustain, protract, postpone, defer, continue.

ant – curtail.

Propel (verb)

syn – press, push, shove, thrust urge.

ant – pull, stop.

Propitiate (verb)

syn – atone, mediate, intercede, appease, pacify, reconcile, satisfy.

ant – offend.

Prosperity (noun)

syn – success, fortune, affluence, blessings, felicity, happiness, well-being, boom.

ant – adversity.

Protect (verb)

syn – defend, guard, harbour, safeguard, shelter, shield, pamper.

ant – attack, plunder.

Prototype (noun)

syn – original, paradigm, precedent, example, archetype, protoplast, ideal.

ant – duplicate, counterpart.

Proverb (noun)

syn – adage, aphorism, epigram, maxim, motto, saying.

Prowess (noun)

syn – bravery, courage, gallantry, daring, valour, intrepidity, heroism, fearlessness.

ant – cowardice, incompetence.

Proxy (noun)

syn – substitude, agent, delegate, representative

Pseudonym (noun)

syn – alisa, penname.

Psychotic (adjective)

syn – demented, deranged, insane, mad, lunatic, psychopathic.

ant – sane, sensible.

Puerile (adjective)

syn – boyish, childish, youthful, foolish, weak, petty, frivolous, trifling, trivial, senseless.

ant – adult, mature.

Pull (verb)

syn – drag, draw, haul, tug, yank.

ant – push, propel.

Pummel (noun/verb)

syn – beat, strike, knob, hit, punch, whack, thrash, flog, bang, thump, cudgel, bruise.

Purge (verb)

syn – cleanse, purify, evacuate, absolve, pardon, scour, wash away.

ant – defile, desecrate.

Purpose (noun/verb)

syn – aim, end, goal, object, objective, intent, plan, project.

Puzzle (noun/verb)

syn – riddle, problem, mystery, enigma, conundrum, perplex.

ant – clarify.

Q 

Quail (verb/noun)

syn – cower, shrink, quake, tremble, flinch, faint, type of bird.

ant – courageous.

Quaint (adjective)

syn – strange, queer, curious, uncommon, singular, extraordinary, unique, fanciful, odd, affected, old-fashioned, archaic, antique.

ant – ordinary, modern.

Qualify (verb)

syn – fit, adapt, modify, equip, entitle, prepare, ease, limit, restrict, soften, abate, moderate, vary, temper, modulate, affect, dilute.

ant – disqualify.

Qualm (noun)

syn – pang, agony, sickness, twinge, scruple, remorse, compunction, uneqsiness.

ant – ease.

Quandary (noun)

syn – difficulty, predicament, corner, perplexity, bewilderment, strait, dilemma.

Quantity (noun)

syn – amount, number, total, composite.

Quash (verb)

syn – crush, beat, subdue, suppress, stop, repress, annul, nullify, cancel, invalidate, abate.

Queasy (adjective)

syn – sick, nauseated, squeamish, qualmish, sensitive, delicate.

Queer (adjective)

syn – crazy, funny, odd, peculiar.

ant – ordinary, commonplace.

Quell (verb)

syn – calm, placate, subdue, suppress, tranquilize, overcome, overpower, still, compose, assuage, mitigate, allay, appease, dull, soothe, blunt.

ant – provoke, incite.

Quench (verb)

syn – extinguish, stifle, repress, satiate, appease, slake, allay.

ant – thirst.

Query (verb/noun)

syn – question, inquiry, problem, doubt, dispute.

ant – answer, accept.

Quibble (noun)

syn – evasion, pun, clinch, pretence, quirk, shift, cavil, subterfuge, prevarication.

Quick (adjective/noun)

syn – rapid, swift, fast, precipitate, precipitous.

ant – slow, listless.

Quicken (verb)

syn – expedite, hurry, rush, speed, hasten, accelerate.

ant – slow, delay.

Quiescence (noun)

syn – rest, repose, silence, quiet, remission, calm, peace, tranquility.

ant – agitation, excitement.

Quip (noun)

syn – jest, repartee, sally, taunt, gibe, jeer, scoff, sneer, mock, crank, witticism.

Quirk (noun)

syn – peculiarity, twist.

Quiver (verb/noun)

syn – trembling, shake, tremble, shudder, shiver, vibrate, oscillate, palpitate, flutter, twitch, flicker.

Quota (noun)

syn – share, contingent, proportion, allotment, part, apportionment, quantity, proportional.

Quotation (noun)

syn – citation, extract, selection, cutting, clipping rate, current price.

Quote (verb)

syn – cite, adduce, excerpt, instance, name, extract.

R 

Rabble (noun)

syn – mob, rout, scum, trash, masses, riff-raff, disorderly crowd, populace, incoherent, discourse, medley.

ant – elite, aristocracy.

Rabid (adjective)

syn – raging, mad, furious, frantic, rampant, fanatical, intolerant.

ant – rational.

Raid (noun)

syn – foray, sortie, invasion, incursion, plunder.

ant – protect, secure.

Raillery (noun)

syn – teasing, ridicule, mockery, make fun, good-humoured ragging, jeer, sneer.

ant – scoff, criticise, condemn.

Raise (noun/verb)

syn – elavate, hoist, lift, promote, uplift, escalate.

ant – lower, descend, depress, demote.

Ramify (verb)

syn – separate, branch, extend, divide.

ant – unite, integrate.

Rancour (noun)

syn – anger, fury, resentment, hatred, enmity, animosity, gall, grudge, spite, ill-will.

ant – benevolence, affection.

Random (adjective/ noun)

syn – casual, desultory, haphazard, chance, irregular, aimless, erratic.

ant – systematic, orderly.

Raven (adjective/verb)

syn – black, inky, sable, ebony, devour, eat, prey, greedy, rapacious.

ant – sated, satiated.

Reach (verb/noun)

syn – accomplish, achieve, attain, earn, come, get, arrive.

ant – depart, miss, fail.

Read (verb)

syn – browse, devour, leaf, peruse, scan.

ant – write.

Rebound (verb/noun)

syn – reverberate, retaliate, recoil, react, ricochet, repercussion, kick, rebut.

Rebuke (verb)

syn – admonish, censure, reprimand, reprove, reproach, admonish, upbraid, chide.

ant – commend, praise, acclaim.

Recapitulate (verb)

syn – repeat, review, summarise, recite, rehearse.

ant – narrate.

Receptacle (noun)

syn – depository, receiver, container, bin, vessel, well, case, reservoir.

ant – donor.

Reciprocal (adjective)

syn – mutual, alternate, complementary, correspondent, correlative.

ant – one-sided.

Reckless (adjective)

syn – daredevil, foolhardy, rash, adventurous.

ant – cautious, wary.

Reckoning (noun)

syn – consideration, estimate, account, scope, charge, esteem, arrangement, settlement.

Recommend (verb)

syn – advise, advocate, counsel, prescribe, suggest.

ant – disapprove, discourage.

Recompense (verb/noun)

syn – reward, repay, compensate, renumerate, redress, reimburse, redeem, reward, satisfaction, indemnify, requite.

ant – penalty.

Recover (verb)

syn – reclaim, recoup, regain, restore, retrieve, recuperate, repair.

ant – lose, mislay, deteriorate.

Rectitude (noun)

syn – integrity, honesty, justice, equity, virtue, correct, uprightness, righteousness, straightforwardness.

ant – laxity, corruption.

Recumbent (adjective)

syn – leaning, reclining, prostrate, reposing, idle, inactive, listless.

ant – erect, active.

Reduce (verb)

syn – abate, curtail, diminish, lower, decrease, mane, weaken.

ant – raise, enhance, increase.

Redundant (adjective)

syn – surplus, unnecessary, needless, useless, copious, superfluous, plentiful, inordinate, diffuse, tautological, verbose, wordy.

ant – essential, terse.

Reek (noun/verb)

syn – smoke, steam, exhale, smell, fume, stack, vapour, effluvium.

ant – perfume.

Refined (adjective)

syn – purified, clarified, cultivated, civilized, fine, polite, stylish, accomplished, gracious, classic, exquisite, pure.

ant – coarse, crude.

Refreshing (adjective)

syn – reviving, pleasant, cooling, invigorating, grateful, animating.

ant – wearisome, tiring, exhausting, draining.

Refuge (noun)

syn – shelter, retreat, sanctuary, stronghold, harbour, safety, security, protection, resort, asylum.

ant – exposure.

Refund (verb)

syn – repay, reimburse, restore, return.

ant – withold.

Regale (verb/noun)

syn – entertain, refresh,

gratify, feast, banquet, delight, sumptuous repast.

ant – bore.

Regenerate (verb/ adjective)

syn – revive, generate, anew, convert, renew, change, reproduce, convert, born again.

ant – degenerate.

Rehabilitate (verb)

syn – reinstate, restore, reestablish, renew, repair, reintegrate, reconstruct, renovate.

ant – displace.

Reject (verb/noun)

syn – decline, refuse, repudiate, spurn, knock back, turn down, discard.

ant – accept, acknowledge.

Religious (adjective)

syn – devout, pious, reverent, sanctimonious, sacred, faithful.

ant – atheist, impious.

Relinquish (verb)

syn – abdicate, cede, renounce, resign, surrender, yield, leave, quit, vacate, resign, forsake, forswear, forego, waive, abandon.

ant – claim, possess.

Remain (verb)

syn – abide, tarry, stay, linger, continue.

ant – leave, depart.

Remarkable (adjective)

syn – noticeable, observable, singular, famous, rare, prominent, wonderful, striking, distinguished, extraordinary, uncommon, conscious.

ant – ordinary, usual.

Remember (verb)

syn – memorize, recall, recollect, remind, retain, reminisce, review.

ant – forget, suppress.

Remove (verb/noun)

syn – dismiss, eject, evict, oust, expel, sack, eliminate, distance.

ant – retain, possess.

Renegade (noun)

syn – criminal, crook, desperado, gangster, gunman thug, mobster, hoodlum, outlaw, vagabond, deserter, rebel, traitor.

ant – saint, patriot.

Renewal (noun)

syn – rebirth, rejuvenation, renaissance, refresh, revive, extension.

ant – degenerate.

Renounce (verb)

syn – reject, deny, decline, disclaim, abjure, quit, repudiate, forswear, abnegate, relinquish, forego, resign, desert, surrender.

ant – claim, possess.

Repair (verb/noun)

syn – correct, fix, mend, rectify, remedy, renovate, conserve, revise, make up for.

ant – break, destroy, damage.

Repartee (noun)

syn – retort, witty, rejoinder, banter.

Replace (verb)

syn – displace, supersede, supplant, change.

ant – conserve, maintain.

Replenish (verb)

syn – fill, stock, refill, renew, supply, provide, furnish, store, enrich.

ant – deplete, exhaust.

Replete (adjective)

syn – full, abounding, well-stocked, fraught, charged, well-provided.

ant – deficient, lacking.

Reprehensible (adjective)

syn – blameworthy, culpable, deplorable, opprobrious, regrettable.

ant – admirable, praiseworthy, commendable.

Representative (noun)

syn – agent, delegate, deputy, proxy, stand-in, substitute, understudy.

Reprieve (verb/noun)

syn – respite, delay, relieve, pardon, remission.

ant – penalty, punishment.

Repulsive (adjective)

syn – abhorrent, abominable, disgusting, loathsome, repellent, repugnant, revolting.

ant – attractive, pleasing.

Reputation (noun)

syn – name, fame, character, credit, repute, regard, estimation, respect, esteem, renown, honour, prestige, distinction, éclat.

ant – notoriety.

Request (verb/noun)

syn – appeal, application, invitation, petition, requisitions, apply, ask, invite, seek, solicit.

ant – command, order.

Require (verb)

syn – want, wish for, lack, need, yearn, long.

ant – get, possess.

Resentment (noun)

syn – huff, offence, pique, umbrage.

ant – admiration, affection.

Resilient (adjective)

syn – buoyant, rebounding, elastic, springy.

ant – static, fixed.

Reside (verb)

syn – dwell, inhabit, live, occupy, settle.

Resolution (noun)

syn – decision, determination, resolve.

ant – hesitation, doubt, vacillation.

Resound (verb)

syn – echo, reverberate, ring, extol, sound, praise.

ant – quiet, still.

Respect (noun)

syn – honour, regard, esteem, deference, reverence, consideration, veneration.

ant – contempt, disrespect.

Resplendent (adjective)

syn – brilliant, splendid, shining, radiant, beaming, luminous, bright, lucid, glorious, glittering.

ant – dull, sombre.

Result (noun/verb)

syn – consequence, effect, outcome, denounment, finish.

ant – cause, origin, initial.

Retaliate (verb)

syn – return, repay, revenge, retort, match, avenge, requite, pay back.

ant – forgive, overlook.

Retired (adjective)

syn – withdrawn, apart, secret, private, sequestered, solitary, secluded, abstracted, superannuated.

ant – active.

Revelry (noun)

syn – carousal, rout, revel, festivity, orgy, riot, bacchanal.

ant – mourning, sobriety.

Revere (verb)

syn – adore, idolize, reverence, venerate, worship.

ant – condemn, blaspheme, despise.

Revive (verb)

syn – rouse, quicken, reanimate, revitalize, invigorate, recover, refresh, restore, strengthen, recall.

ant – destroy.

Ridicule (noun/verb)

syn – mockery, sarcasm, irony, derision, satire.

ant – respect, regard, praise.

Rigid (adjective)

syn – stiff, inflexible, firm, unyielding, erect, sharp, stern, harsh, austere, bristling, rigorous.

ant – flexible, pliant.

Rightful (adjective)

syn – due, deserved, fair, equitable, just, merited, well-earned, lawful, right, moral.

ant – wrongful, improper.

Riotous (adjective)

syn – chaotic, anarchic, disorganized, unruly, tumultuous, revelling, wanton, merry, unrestrained, boisterous, seditious.

ant – dull, sombre, funereal.

Rite (noun)

syn – ceremony, liturgy, ritual, observance.

Rivalry (noun)

syn – competition, strife, contention, race, contest.

ant – camaraderie.

Robbery (noun)

syn – burglary, larceny, mugging, theft, thuggery, stick-up, cheating, stealing.

Robust (adjective)

syn – strong, healthy, athletic, stout, sinewy, hale, muscular, energetic, hardy, sturdy, brawny.

ant – weakling, sickly.

Roguish (adjective)

syn – rascally, scoundrel, dishonest, knave, puckish, wanton, mischievous.

ant – honest, sincere.

Rot (verb/noun)

syn – decay, decompose, moulder, putrefy, spoil.

ant – bloom, flourish.

Rotate (verb)

syn – gyrate, revolve, roll, spin, turn, twirl, whirl.

ant – standstill.

Rough (noun/verb)

syn – bumpy, corrugated, crenellated, crooked, rugged, jagged, serrated, uneven.

ant – smooth, fine.

Rout (noun/verb)

syn – defeat, uproar, brawl, discomfit, rabble, overthrow, fight, roar, disturbance, noise.

ant – peace, victory.

Ruminate (verb)

syn – think, meditate, muse, chew, reflect, brood, ponder, cogitate.

ant – act.

Rumple (verb/noun)

syn – wrinkle, crumple, pucker, disarrange, dishevel, crease, crush, corrugate, muss, fold.

ant – straighten, ironed.

Run (verb)

syn – canter, gallop, jog, lope, pace, race, sprint, trot.

ant – stop, saunter, amble.

Rupture (noun/verb)

syn – breach, split, fracture, disruption, feud, break, faction, contention, schism, burst.

ant – mend, build.

Ruse (noun)

syn – trick, hile, hoax, fraud, deceit, imposture, sham, stratagem.

Rustic (adjective/noun)

syn – rural, simple, plain, loutish, uncouth, plain, peasant, boor, bumpkin, countryman.

S

Sacred (adjective)

syn – blessed, divine, hallowed, consecrated, holy.

ant – desecrated, profane.

Sad (adjective)

syn – blue, dejected, depressed, despondent, downcast, melancholy, lugubrious, disconsolate, gloomy.

ant – happy, joyous, exhilarated.

Sagacious (adjective)

syn – astute, intelligent, discerning, rational, acute, keen, able penetrating, perspicacious sapient.

ant – stupid, obtuse.

Salary (noun)

syn – fee, pay, emolument, stipend, wage, remuneration, honorarium.

Sample (noun/verb)

syn – case, example, instance, specimen, illustration.

Sanction (verb)

syn – ratify, confirm, penalty, punishment, support, endorse, warrant, legalise, bind, authority.

ant – prohibition, ban.

Sanguine (adjective/verb)

syn – confident, hopeful, enthusiastic, animated, red, cheerful, warm, ardent, lively, buoyant.

ant – pessimistic, pale.

Sanitate (verb)

syn – decontaminate, disinfect, sanitize, fumigate, sterilize.

ant – pollute.

Sarcastic (adjective)

syn – biting, caustic, cutting, sardonic, contemptuous.

ant – complimentary, flattering.

Satanic (adjective)

syn – evil, fiendish, wicked, devilish, malicious, diabolical.

ant – saintly, heavenly.

Satire (noun)

syn – sarcasm, diatribe, squib, lampoon, ridicule, irony, invective, burlesque.

ant – flattery, praise.

Satisfy (verb)

syn – ease, fill, palliate, meet, fulfill, convince.

ant – dissatisfy.

Saturnine (adjective)

syn – dull, morose, sombre, leaden, dark, dull, heavy, grave, sad, gloomy.

ant – sanguine, jovial.

Saunter (verb)

syn – loiter, linger, lounge, stroll, dawdle, lag, delay, move slowly.

ant – jog, trot.

Save (verb/preposition)

syn – deliver, ransom, redeem, rescue, conserve, help, recover, repair, except.

ant – destroy, harm, spend.

Savoury (adjective/noun)

syn – relishing, spicy, tangy, pungent, piquant, luscious, delicious, nice, tasty.

ant – insipid, tasteless, bland.

Say (verb)

syn – speak, communicate, state, verbalize, tell, utter.

ant – quiet, withhold.

Scanty (adjective)

syn – inadequate, meagre, scarce, insufficient, skimpy, sparse.

ant – sufficient, adequate.

Scatter (verb)

syn – broadcast, diffuse, disperse, disseminate, spread, permeate.

ant – gather, unite.

Sceptic (adjective)

syn – doubter, agnostic, atheist, free thinker, unbeliever.

ant – bigot, zealot, believer.

Scintillate (verb)

syn – sparkle, twinkle, glitter, flash, emit sparks.

ant – fuse, dull.

Scoff (verb)

syn – gibe, jeer, poke fun, sneer contempt, taunt.

ant – praise, commend.

Scold (verb)

syn – berate, chide, upbraid, tell off, tick off, rebuke.

ant – praise, compliment.

Scoop (noun/verb)

syn – spoon, shovel, ladle, dig, bail.

Scoundrel (noun)

syn – cad, heel, knave, rogue, villain, rascal, scamp, scallywag.

ant – gentleman.

Scour (verb)

syn – clean, scrape, rake, cleanse, brighten, scrub, efface, course, career, scamper.

ant – sell, stain.

Scourge (noun/verb)

syn – whip, lash, punishment, curse, affliction, plague, nuisance, chastise, afflict, harass, torment.

ant – blessing, indulge.

Scramble (verb/noun)

syn – struggle, strive, clamber, climb, contest.

ant – dawdle.

Scrutiny (noun)

syn – search, inspection, examination, inquisition, inquiry, exploration, sifting.

ant – ignorance.

Scurrilous (adjective)

syn – abusive, insolent, reproachful, vituperative, opprobrious, contumelious, ribald, offensive.

ant – deferential, polite.

Section (noun)

syn – area, locale, locality, neighbourhood, quarter, region.

Sedate (adjective)

syn – calm, composed, placid, tranquil, collected, cool, still, sober, serious, grave, thoughtful, staid, earnest, solemn, imperturbable.

ant – frivolous, flighty, jaunty.

Sedition (noun)

syn – riot, rising, rebellion,

treason, revolt, tumult, uprising, mutiny, roar, insurgence.

ant – peace, amity.

See (verb/noun)

syn – inspect, look, notice, observe, regard, watch, witness, perceive, examine, study, imagine.

ant – overlook, ignore.

Seemly (adjective)

syn – fit, befitting, becoming, covenient, suitable, expedient, appropriate, decorous, beautiful, good-looking, graceful.

ant – unseemly, ungainly, awkward.

Send (verb)

syn – deliver, dispatch, forward, ship, transmit.

ant – receive, retain.

Sensation (noun)

syn – feeling, idea, sense, percept, perception, emotion.

ant – apathy, insenstivity.

Sensible (adjective)

syn – lucid, rational, reasonable, sane.

ant – foolish, unreasonable.

Sentiment (noun)

syn – feeling, thought, opinion, notion, emotion, tenderness, disposition, saying, maxim, remark.

ant – reason, logic.

Sentimental (adjective)

syn – effusive, gushing, maudlin, mawkish, mushy, maudlin, romantic, sloppy, slushy.

ant – cynical, imperturbable.

Separate (verb/ adjective)

syn – detach, disconnect, dismember, disunite, disengage, break, divide, sever.

ant – connect, consolidate.

Sequence (noun)

syn – arrangement, progression, series, succession, gradation.

ant – disorganised, disorder.

Sequester (verb)

syn – separate, remove, put aside, withdraw, seclude.

ant – public, socialize.

Serpentine (adjective)

syn – winding, meandering, crooked, spiral, undulating, sinuous, twisted.

ant – straight.

Sever (verb)

syn – break, disrupt, separate, split, sunder, cleave, divide, hew, tear.

ant – connect, unite.

Several (adjective)

syn – diverse, various, many, sundry.

ant – none, one.

Shackle (noun)

syn – restraint, chain, fetter, handcuff, manacle, tether.

ant – extricate, liberate.

Shaft (noun)

syn – thill, pole, arrow, missile, handle, trunk, axis, spindle, stem, stalk, spire, pinnacle.

Shake (verb/noun)

syn – quake, quiver, shiver, shudder, tremble, totter, vibrate.

ant – quieten, still.

Sham (verb)

syn – feign, pretend, trick, cheat, delude, dupe, fake, deceive, impose, ape, mock, phony, bogus.

ant – genuine, real.

Shame (noun/verb)

syn – mortify, embarrass, abash, faze, discomfit, rattle.

ant – pride, honour.

Shameful (adjective)

syn – disgraceful, dishonourable, ignominious, scandalous.

ant – exemplary, ideal, upright, honourable.

Share (noun)

syn – partake, participate, join, commune, relate.

ant – whole, total.

Shirk (verb)

syn – avoid, cheat, trick, enade, dodge, slink.

ant – welcome.

Shore (noun)

syn – bank, beach, coast, strand, littoral.

Shorten (verb)

syn – abbreviate, abridge, cut, lop, curtail, lessen, reduce.

ant – enlarge, extend.

Show (noun/verb)

syn – display, evince, exhibit, manifest, mean, meaning.

ant – conceal, suppress.

Showy (adjective)

syn – colourful, ostentatious, loud, garish, gaudy, vulgar, affected.

ant – humble, simple, unfaffected.

Shrew (noun)

syn – harridan, termagant, virago, vixen.

ant – angel, saintly.

Shrewd (adjective)

syn – artful, sly, cunning, wily, crafty, acute, sharp, penetrating, discerning, discriminating.

ant – obtuse, stupid.

Sickness (noun)

syn – ailment, complaint, illness, disease, disorder, malaise, malady, infirmity.

ant – health, well-being.

Signal (noun/adjective)

syn – token, mark, sign, cue, indication, notable, remarkable, conspicuous.

Significant (adjective)

syn – grave, important, meaningful, consequential, serious, vital, weighty, momentous, crucial.

ant – insignificant, trivial.

Silly (adjective)

syn – senseless, absurd, trifling, simple, foolish, inept, brainless, shallow, indiscreet, impudent.

ant – sensible.

Similar (adjective)

syn – alike, comparable, parallel, counterpart, copy, duplicate.

ant – different, contradictory.

Simple (adjective)

syn – easy, facile, simplified, effortless, elementary, basic, uncomplicated, plain, unaffected, modest, unostentatious.

ant – complex, intricate.

Simulate (verb)

syn – feign, ape, make-believe, pretend, assume, mimic.

ant – reality, factual.

Sin (noun)

syn – error, fault, indiscretion, misdeed, wrong, transgression, crime, flaw, unethical.

ant – goodness, benefaction.

Sincere (adjective)

syn – genuine, honest, open, unfeigned, whole hearted, heartfelt, truthful.

ant – dishonest, insincere.

Sinewy (adjective)

syn – brawny, muscular, vigorous, stalwart, strapping, robust, powerful, able-bodied.

ant – puny, emaciated.

Siren (noun/adjective)

syn – tempter, seducer, bewitching, alluring, fascinat ing.

Site (noun)

syn – location, place, point, scene, setting, spot, section.

Size (noun)

syn – area, bulk, expanse, extent, mass, scope, volume.

Skeptical (adjective)

syn – doubter, questioning, incredulous, unbelieving.

ant – believer.

Skill (noun)

syn – adroitness, artistry, deftness, finesse, flair, mastery, acumen, aptitude.

ant – incompetence.

Skip (verb/noun)

syn – bound, leave out, leap, spring.

ant – crawl.

Slave (noun/verb)

syn – peon, serf, thrall, vassal, bondman.

ant – master, lord.

Slovenly (adjective)

syn – untidy, unclean, disorderly, loose, lazy, unkempt, perfunctory, negligent.

ant – neat, organized.

Sluggish (adjective)

syn – idle, lazy, inactive, slothful, indolent, slow, tame, stupid, supine, inert.

ant – active, quick.

Sloth (noun)

syn – apathy, catatonia, indolence, laziness, listlessness, inertia, inactive, uninvolved.

ant – activity, industry.

Slow (adjective)

syn – deliberate, dilatory, gradual, laggard, leisurely, retarded, slack, sluggish.

ant – fast, agile, quick.

Small (adjective)

syn – little, short, tiny, wee, squat, petite, diminutive.

ant – big, large.

Smell (verb/noun)

syn – aroma, bouquet, odour, fragrance, perfume, scent, stench, stink.

Smile (noun/verb)

syn – grin, leer, simper, smirk, laugh.

ant – frown, fury.

Snare (noun/verb)

syn – entrap, entangle, catch, ensnare, noose, net, trap, wile.

ant – liberate, free.

Sneak (verb/noun)

syn – skulk, lurk, steal, slink, truckle, lurker, mean person, sly.

Snug (adjective)

syn – close, comfortable, convenient, compact, neat, trim.

ant – exposed.

Sodality (noun)

syn – fraternity, brotherhood, society, fellowship.

Soil (noun/verb)

syn – dirty, besmirch, omudge, sully, pollute, discolour.

ant – clean, purify.

Sojourn (verb/noun)

syn – abide, stay, lodge, remain, live, dwell, put up, temporary abode residence.

ant – travel.

Solace (noun/verb)

syn – comfort, consolation, cheer, relief, soothe, allay, soften, mitigate, kelieve, assuage.

ant – distress, afflict.

Solicitude (noun)

syn – anxiety, concern, worry, care, trouble, perplexity, carefulness.

ant – aloofness, indifference.

Solitude (noun)

syn – isolation, seclusion, loveliness, retirement, privacy, wilderness, waste, lonely place, deserted region.

ant – society, company.

Sonorous (adjective)

syn – sounding, resonant, resounding, high-sounding, loud, ringing, full-toned.

ant – soft, mellow.

Soup (noun/verb)

syn – broth, stew, stock, potage, chowder, bouillon, consommé, in tight spot, in problem.

Sour (adjective)

syn – acid, acrid, bitter, caustic, tart, sarcastic, savoury, vindictive, pungent.

ant – sweet, bland.

Sparkling (adjective)

syn – flashing, flickering, glimmering, glittering, luminous, scintillating, shimmering, twinkling, bright.

ant – dull, lackluster.

Sparse (adjective)

syn – scattered, infrequent, sporadic, dispersed, thin.

ant – dense.

Spasm (noun)

syn – fit, poroxysm, twitch, cramp, crick, throe, seizure.

Species (noun)

syn – group, kind, class, collection, description, variety, form, fashion, shape.

Specific (adjective/noun)

syn – definite, explicit, express, accurate, clear, conclusive.

ant – vague, ambiguous, obscure, general.

Spectator (noun)

syn – onlooker, audience, viewer, observer, voyeur, witness, beholder, bystander.

ant – performer, participant.

Spectre (noun)

syn – ghost, apparition, spirit, sprite, shadow, goblin, wraith, banshee.

Speculate (verb)

syn – meditate, contemplate, cogitate, reflect, ponder, muse, ruminate, think, consider, theorise.

ant – know, knowledge.

Speech (noun)

syn – lecture, sermon, discourse, address, homily, oration, harangue, spiel, conversation.

ant – silence.

Speed (noun/verb)

syn – alacrity, celerity, haste, hurry, promptness, velocity, dispatch, swiftness.

ant – delay, languor.

Spirited (adjective)

syn – animated, lively, vivacious, brisk, active, bold, courageous, ardent, earnest, sprightly, frisky.

ant – apathetic, listless.

Spite (noun/verb)

syn – malice, malevolence, rancour, venom, gall, spleen, vindictiveness, grudge, pique, offend, vex, annoy, mortify, thwart, injure, ill-will.

ant – benevolence.

Spontaneous (adjective)

syn – impromptur, improvised, unreheansed, unplanned, impulsive, extemporaneous, unpremeditated.

ant – rehearsed, forced.

Spur (noun/verb)

syn – goad, needle, sting, nag, stimulus, suddenly, inspiration.

ant – quell, stop, block.

Spurious (adjective)

syn – false, insincere, counterfeit, forged, shoddy, snide, counterfeit, deceitful, sham, feigned, fictitious, adulterate.

ant – authentic, genuine.

Spurt (noun/verb)

syn – jet, sudden gush, spout, well, spring out.

ant – drip.

Squall (verb/noun)

syn – cry, bawl, yell, scream, outcry, storm, blast, gust, gale, storm, blast, flurry, tempest, hurricane.

Squeal (verb/noun)

syn – caw, cheep, chirp, coo, hoot, peep, screech, squawk, squeak.

Squelch (verb)

syn – suppress, silence, crush, quash, quieten, subdue.

ant – provoke, arouse.

Staid (adjective)

syn – sober, grave, steady, composed, demure, solemn, calm, sedate, serious.

ant – frivolous, flighty.

Stamina (noun)

syn – strength, vigour, force, stoutness, power, lustiness, sturdiness.

ant – weakness.

Steal (verb)

syn – filch, heist, lift, nick,

pilfer, pinch, purloin, snitch, send off, swipe, souvenir.

ant – restore.

Standard (noun/adjective)

syn – criterion, gauge, measure, test, touchstone, yardstick.

ant – irregular.

Stealthy (adjective)

syn – clandestine, furtive, sneaky, surreptitious, sly, underhand.

ant – overt, declared, obvious.

Steep (adjective/verb/ noun)

syn – abrupt, sheer, precipitous.

ant – flat, level, low.

Sterile (adjective)

syn – barren, arid, infertile, unfruitful, unproductive, childless, infecund, dry.

ant – fertile, productive.

Stick (noun/verb)

syn – adhere, cleave, cling, cohere, connect, tie.

ant – sever, separate.

Stigma (noun)

syn – stain, blot, disgrace, reproach, dishonour, shame, spot, blur, brand, tarnish, taint.

Stimulate (verb)

syn – enliven, excite, galvanize, titillate, whet.

ant – deaden, quell.

Stint (noun/verb)

syn – assignment, chore, duty, job, task, obligation.

ant – hobby.

Stomach (noun/verb)

syn – abdomen, belly, guts, tummy, liking, endure, tolerate.

Stop (verb/noun)

syn – cease, desist, halt, quit, arrest, block, check, discontinue, prevent.

ant – begin.

Stratagem (noun)

syn – article, device, intrigue, wile, fetch, crafty, plot, scheme, artful, ruse, cunning.

Street (noun)

syn – avenue, drive, road, lane, motorway, highway, expressway, clearway, boulevard.

Stroll (verb/noun)

syn – ramble, walk, excursion, trip, tour, roving, wandering, rambling, roam, straggle, range, saunter, loiter, lounge.

ant – run.

Strong (adjective/ adverb)

syn – hardy, muscular, powerful, sturdy, tough, stalwart, healthy.

ant – weak, powerless.

Stubborn (adjective)

syn – adamant, headstrong, obdurate, inflexible, obstinate, pertinacious, pigheaded.

ant – compliant, docile.

Study (noun/verb)

syn – consider, ponder, weigh, contemplate, examine, read, see, think, observe, report, publication.

ant – neglect.

Stupendous (adjective)

syn – astonishing, huge, vast, tremendous, immense, amazing, surprising, astounding, marvellous.

ant – ordinary.

Stupid (adjective)

syn – dull, dumb, obtuse, slow, retarded, asinine, dense, thick, unintelligent, blockhead.

ant – clever, bright.

Stupor (noun)

syn – lethargy, numbness, coma, daze, confusion, stupefaction.

Stylish (adjective)

syn – chic, dapper, fashionable, modish, smart, spruce, artistic, elegant, exquisite, orderly, vogue.

ant – dowdy, unkempt.

Suave (adjective)

syn – pleasant, agreeable, urbane, debonair, affable, gracious, courteous, smooth, glib, unctuous.

ant – rude, coarse.

Subdue (verb)

syn – check, constrain, curb, inhibit, repress, restrain, suppress, control, surmount.

ant – provoke, incite, stimulate.

Sublime (adjective/ noun)

syn – high, elevated, exalted, great, grand, lofty, aloft, noble, stately, majestic, eminent, august, raised, refine, heighten, idealise.

ant – ridiculous, farcical.

Subsistence (noun)

syn – life, being, entity, support, livelihood, nourishment.

Subterfuge (noun)

syn – evasion, trick, quirk, shuffle, pretence, pretext, mask, sophistry.

ant – honesty.

Succinct (adjective)

syn - short, brief, concise, terse, curt, pithy, compact, laconic, condensed, summary.

ant – prolix.

Succour (verb/noun)

syn – aid, assist, help, relieve, cherish, foster, help, nurse, comfort, encourage, support.

ant – torment, torture.

Succumb (verb)

syn – yield, submit, capitulate, give in, die, surrender.

ant – resist.

Summary (noun)

syn – abstract, digest, outline, précis, synopsis, terse, abridgement, shorten.

ant – amplification, lengthy.

Summit (noun)

syn – acme, apex, climax, peak, pinnacle, zenith.

ant – base, nadir.

Summon (verb)

syn – beckon, call, conjure, invoke, send for, subpoena, name, request.

ant – dismiss.

Supercilious (adjective)

syn – haughty, overbearing, disdainful, proud, arrogant, snobbish, contemptuous, dictatorial, lordly, magisterial, imperious.

ant – humble.

Superficial (adjective)

syn – flat, obvious, shallow, external, outward, outside, slight, meretricious, frivolous, banal, bland.

ant – profound, genuine.

Supernatural (adjective)

syn – magical, miraculous, bizarre, mystical, queer, unusual.

ant – earthly, wordly.

Supersede (verb)

syn – suspend, annul, displace, replace, supplant, succeed, remove, obviate, neutralize.

ant – irreplaceable.

Supple (adjective)

syn – agile, limber, lithe, nimble, resilient, spry, malleable, adaptable.

ant – clumsy, heavy, stiff.

Supporter (noun)

syn – adherent, disciple, follower, partisan, assistant.

ant – opponent, antagonist.

Suppose (verb)

syn – assume, guess, conjecture, surmise, postulate, imagine, mean.

ant – know, prove, validate.

Sure (adjective/adverb)

syn – certain, definite, doubtless, specific, clear, positive.

ant – unsure, doubtful.

Surfeit (verb)

syn – cloy, pall, sate, dull, glut, satiate, cram, gorge.

ant – deficiency, starve.

Surprised (noun/verb)

syn – amazed, astonished, astounded, flabbergasted, stunned, confused, puzzled, upset.

ant – imperturbable.

Surreptitious (adjective)

syn – introduced, hidden, secret, stealthy, fraudulently.

ant – overt, obvious, apparent.

Susceptible (adjective)

syn – sensitive, excitable, receptive, capable, inclined, predisposed, impressionable.

ant – rigid, fixed.

Suspicion (noun)

syn – surmise, doubt, conjecture, hint, trace, guess, assumption, distrust, misgiving, apprehension, fear.

ant – trust.

Swarthy (adjective)

syn – black, coloured, dusky, tanned, tawny, mulatto.

ant – fair, light-skinned, pale.

Swell (verb/noun)

syn – bulge, dilate, distend, inflate, enlarge, extend.

ant – deflate, depress.

Swindler (noun/verb)

syn – knave, rogue, cheat, fraud, embezzler, impostor, trickster, fake, forger, defaulter.

ant – honest.

Sycophant (noun)

syn – parasite, flatterer, fawner, toady, hanger-on.

ant – sincere, genuine, critic.

Symbol (noun)

syn – badge, device, emblem, hallmark, sign, token, meaning.

Sympathy (noun)

syn – pity, tenderness, affinity, accord, communion, compassion, commiseration.

ant – antipathy, indifference.

Symptom (noun)

syn – indication, sign, mark, clue, syndrome, diagnostic, token, prognostic.

Synopsis (noun)

syn – epitome, abstract, compend, compendium, outline, summary, digest, general view, abridgement.

Systematic (adjective)

syn – methodical, orderly, regular, formal, method.

ant – disorganized, chaotic, random.

T

Taboo (noun/verb/adjective)

syn – forbid, prohibit, inviolable, interdict.

ant – permitted.

Taciturn (adjective)

syn – silent, reserved, close, reticent, uncommunicative, timid, mum, dumb, laconic.

ant – verbose, talkative, garrulous, loquacious.

Taint (verb/noun)

syn – corrupt, infect, contaminate, poison, defile, putrefy, pollute, spoil, disease, vitiate, tarnish, stain, sully, fault, blemish, flaw, spot, defect.

ant – purify.

Talent (noun)

syn – gift, skill, ability, turn, aptitude, faculty, capacity, genius, knack, forte.

ant – inability.

Tally (noun/verb)

syn – match, correspond, agree, counterpart, muster, conform, harmonise, square, coincide, suit.

ant – clash.

Tardy (adjective)

syn – slow, sluggish, dilatory, slack, late, overdue, backward, slow.

ant – prompt.

Tarnish (verb/noun)

syn – soil, stain, sully, slur, defame, smear, smudge, dim, discolour, dull, blemish, blot.

ant – polish.

Tasty (adjective)

syn – delicious palatable, toothsome.

ant – bland, unappetizing.

Tautology (noun)

syn – repetition, reiteration, verbosity, wordiness, redundancy.

ant – conciseness, terseness.

Tawdry (adjective)

syn – gaudy, showy, flashy, glittering, garish, loud.

ant – sober, tasteful.

Teach (verb)

syn – coach, educate, indoctrinate, instruct, school, train, tutor, study.

ant – learn.

Tear (verb/noun)

syn – rend, rip, rive, cut, sever.

ant – connect, repair.

Teem (verb)

syn – abound, overflow, swarm, flow, prevalent.

ant – vacate, wane.

Tell (verb)

syn – convey, impart, narrate, recite, recount, relate, report, speak, utter.

ant – listen.

Temperament (noun)

syn – character, disposition, nature, personality.

Temporary (adjective)

syn – ephemeral, fleeting, momentary, passing, transient, transitory.

ant – permanent, everlasting.

Tempt (verb)

syn – allure, attract, beguile, entice, lure, seduce.

ant – repel, dissuade.

Teanacity (noun)

syn – stubborness, obstinacy, firmness, pertinacity, resolution, doggedness, persistency, strength, perseverance, toughness.

ant – flexibility, fluidity.

Terse (adjective)

syn – concise, brief, laconic, pithy, succinct, compact, sententious, smooth.

ant – tedious, talkative, tautology.

Theatrical (adjective/ noun)

syn – camp, dramatic, flamboyant, histrionic, emotional, passionate.

ant – prosaic, sedate.

Thief (noun)

syn – bandit, brigand, burglar, pirate, robber, gangster.

ant – saint.

Thin (adjective)

syn – lean, scrawny, skinny, slender, slim, spare, willowy, wiry, svelte, bony.

ant – fat.

Think (verb)

syn – cogitate, muse, ponder, deliberate, meditate, reason, reflect, ruminate, speculate, consider, examine, mind, opinion, suppose.

ant – know.

Thoroughbred (adjective)

syn – able, well-educated, accomplished, finished, practiced, qualified, trained, instructed, proficient, genteel.

ant – vagabond, rascal.

Thrift (noun)

syn – frugality, economical, saving.

ant – extravagance.

Thrive (verb)

syn – prosper, succeed, grow, increase, flourish, improve, boom, bloom.

ant – decay, degenerate.

Throng (verb/noun)

syn – crowd, horde, host, mob, multitude, group.

ant – solitary.

Throw (verb)

syn – cast, chuck, fling, heave, hurl, bowl, put, toss, sling, discard.

ant – catch.

Thwart (verb/noun)

syn – frustrate, obstruct, inhibit, foil, balk, hinder.

ant – permit, encourage.

Tie (verb/noun)

syn – bind, fasten, moor, hitch, secure, truss, connect, shackle.

ant – loosen, separate.

Timid (adjective)

syn – bashful, coy, meek, submissive, diffident, shy, timorous, faint-hearted.

ant – bold, daring.

Tip (noun/verb)

syn – lift, turn over, tilt, slant, slope, tapered end, cant, careen, heel, bend, totter.

ant – base, straighten.

Tired (adjective)

syn – beat, fatigued, exhausted, weary, worn out.

ant – invigorated, relaxed, refreshed.

Title (noun/verb)

syn – name, championship, deed, document, appellation.

Toothsome (adjective)

syn – delicious, nice, luscious, dainty, palatable, savoury.

ant – insipid.

Total (noun/adjective)

syn – sum, aggregate, totality, whole, entire, accumulate.

ant – component, part

Torpid (adjective)

syn – numb, lethargic, motionless, sluggish, inert, dull, stupid, listless, sleepy, apathetic

ant – active.

Totter (verb)

syn – lurch, reel, stagger, teeter, wobble, vacillate shake, sway, waver, falter.

ant – steady.

Trail (verb/noun)

syn – draw, drag, trace, follow, hunt, track, mark, footprint, float, creep, hang, grow.

ant – catch.

Training (noun)

syn – drill, discipline, exercise, practise, skill.

Traitor (noun)

syn – betrayer, deserter, rebel, insurgent, revolter, conspirator, renegade.

ant – patriot, loyalist.

Tranquil (adjective)

syn – calm, placid, quiet, serene, still, undisturbed, unruffled, bland.

ant – agitated.

Translucent (adjective)

syn – blurred, filmy, veiled, diaphanous, luminous, vague, opaque.

ant – transparent

Transparent (adjective)

syn – clear, crystalline, limpid, lucid, pellucid, bright.

ant – foggy, obscure, vague.

Transmit (verb)

syn – send, forward, communicate, conduct, radiate, convey, carry.

ant – receive.

Transpire (verb)

syn – happen, appear, occur, disclose, evaporate.

Trash (noun)

syn – dross, refuse, rubbish, waste, worthless, nonsense.

ant – valuable.

Treacherous (adjective)

syn – disloyal, false, hypocritical, specious, betrayer, treasonable, unfaithful.

ant – loyal.

Treat (verb/noun)

syn – cure, heal, mend, remedy, regard, behave, entertain, recover, repair.

ant – neglect.

Tremble (verb)

syn – shake, shudder, shiver, quiver, quake, totter, quaver, rock.

ant – steady.

Trenchant (adjective)

syn – cutting, sharp, incisive, severe, biting, pointed, caustic, pungent, piquant, crisp.

ant – mild, ineffectual.

Trepidation (noun)

syn – trembling, fear, agitation, dismay, alarm, fright, tremor, agitation, consternation.

ant – composure, fearlessness.

Trick (noun/verb)

syn – knack, feat, artifice, blind, dodge, evasion, ruse, manoeuvre, wile, subterfuge, stratagem, cheat, lie, deceive, delude, dupe, hoax, hoodwink, mislead.

ant – honesty, sincerity.

Trite (adjective)

syn – common, banal, stale, worn out, commonplace, stereotyped, hackneyed, threadbare.

ant – creative, original.

Trivial (adjective)

syn – trifling, petty, measly, paltry, puny, insignificant inmaterial, nugatory, small, slight.

ant – significant

Troll (verb/noun)

syn – circulate, sing loudly, allure, entice, catch, sound.

ant – repel.

Troop (noun/verb)

syn – army, forces, personnel, soldiers, come together.

Truant (adjective/ noun)

syn – idler, loiterer, shirk, laggard, absentee, quitter deserter.

ant – present.

Truce (noun)

syn – armistice, peace, cessation, respite, interval, lull, recess, suspension of hostilities.

ant – war.

Trust (noun/verb)

syn – confidence, faith, reliance, dependability

ant – distrust, doubt.

Truthful (adjective)

syn – sincere, true, real, factual, good, honest, candid.

ant – lying, corrupt.

Try (verb/noun)

syn – attempt, strive, endeavour, intend, effort, use, test, strain.

ant – quit, drop.

Tryst (noun)

syn – appointment, meeting, assignation, date, rendezvous.

Tumult (noun)

syn – uproar, turbulence, agitation, confusion, ado, bustle, flurry, racket, turmoil, hubbub, feud, altercation, strife, ferment, disorder.

ant – peace, calm, quiet.

Turbulent (adjective)

syn – blustering, riotous, stormy, tempestuous, wild, tumultous, violent, unruly.

ant – tranquil, placid.

Typical (adjective)

syn – characteristic, indicative, representative, exemplary, model, illustrative, true-to-type.

ant – unlike, eccentric.

Tyranny (noun)

syn – despotism, dictatorship, arbitrary, harshness, oppression, autocracy, cruelty, reign of terror.

ant – democracy.

U 

Ubiquitous (adjective)

syn – omnipresent, universally present.

ant – absent.

Ugly (adjective)

syn – plain, unattractive, unsightly, repulsive bad.

ant – beautiful.

Ulterior (adjective)

syn – farther, indirect, not manifest, remoter, distant

ant – inherent, intrinsic.

Ultimatum (noun)

syn – final condition, last offer.

Ululation (noun)

syn – howl, wail, cry, yelp, bellowing, hoot.

ant – laughter.

Umbrage (noun)

syn – offence, resentment, pique, grudge, shadow.

Unambiguous (adjective)

syn – plain, clear, specific, obvious, apparent, distinct, unmistakable.

ant – obscure, vague.

Unanimous (adjective)

syn – concordant, agreeing, united, harmonious, concurred, consentient.

ant – disagreeing

Unauthentic (adjective)

syn – spurious, insincere, false, sham, feigned, fictitious, counterfeit.

ant – genuine, authentic.

Unbridled (adjective)

syn – unrestrained, reinless, ungovernable, violent, unruly, intractable, lax.

ant – restrained.

Uncanny (adjective)

syn – weird, supernatural, unearthly, spooky, eerie, ghostly.

ant – ordinary.

Uncouth (adjective)

syn – rustic, boorish, awkward, clumsy, inelegant, unsophisticated, loutish, unseemly, unrefined, gawky, ungainly.

ant – refined, polished.

Unctuous (adjective)

syn – greasy, oily, cloying, smooth, bland, fervid, gushing, glib, sycophantic.

ant – sincere.

Undefined (adjective)

syn – indistinct, indefinite, indeterminate, vague.

ant – defined.

Unethical (adjective)

syn – amoral, immoral, unprincipled, unscrupulous, depraved, sinful.

ant – moral, principled.

Undulate (verb)

syn – wave, fluctuate, billow, roll, ripple, pulsate.

ant – steady

Unequivocal (adjective)

syn – indubitable, unmistakable, clear, plain, evident certain, positive, absolute, explicit, partial.

ant – ambiguous.

Unfair (adjective)

syn – unjust, partial, dishonest, dishonorable, unequal, false, oblique.

ant – fair

Unfathomable (adjective)

syn – inscrutable, mysterious, inexplicable, unplumbed, deep, profound, impenetrable.

ant – shallow.

Uninvolved (adjective)

syn – apathetic, bored, indifferent, unconcerned, unmoved.

ant – concerned, interested.

Unite (verb)

syn – blend, combine, fuse, join, knit, merge, coalesce.

ant – scatter.

Unique (adjective)

syn – single, unmatched, singular, uncommon, rare, exceptional, peculiar.

ant – typical, common.

Unlikelihood (noun)

syn – unlikeliness, improbability.

ant – likelihood, probability.

Unobtrusive (adjective)

syn – modest, retiring, unassuming, unpretentious, unostentatious.

ant – pretentious.

Unparalleled (adjective)

syn – modest, retiring, unassuming, unpretentious, unostentatious.

ant – pretentious.

Unparalleled (adjective)

syn – extraordinary, singular, special, unusual, queer.

ant – general, normal.

Unprecedented (adjective)

syn – novel, new, exceptional, without example

ant – precedented, follower.

Unpremeditated (adjective)

syn – extempore, impromptu, spontaneous, unrehearsed, undesigned.

ant – rehearsed.

Unpropitious (adjective)

syn – unfavorable, inauspicious, unpromising, adverse sinister, ill-omened.

ant – favourable, fortune.

Unravel (verb)

syn – untwist, extricate, unfold, evolve, decipher, interpret, disclose.

ant – ravel, complicate.

Unruly (adjective)

syn – intractable, recalcitrant, refractory, restive, uncontrollable, ungovernable, unmanageable, wayward.

ant – compliant, docile.

Unseemly (adjective)

syn – improper, indecorous, unbecoming, unfit, unbefitting, indecent, unsuitable, inappropriate.

ant – proper.

Unsettle (verb)

syn – annoy, irritate, rile, nettle, put out, upset, bother, incite, outrage, anxious, worry.

ant – relieve, calm.

Unshackle (verb)

syn – unchain, loosen, untie, liberate, emancipate, set free, release.

ant – chain, shackle.

Unswerving (adjective)

syn – straight, direct, firm, steady, determined, resolute, stable, constant, unwavering.

ant – unsteady.

Untenable (adjective)

syn – weak, hollow, unsound, unjustifiable, illogical insupportable, fallacious.

ant – sound, logical.

Untimely (adjective/adverb)

syn – immature, mistimed, inopportune, unsuitable, inconvenient, unfortunate, unseasonable.

ant – timely.

Unusual (adjective)

syn – exceptional, rare, unique, off-beat, unparalleled.

ant – common, typical

Unwieldly (adjective)

syn – unmanageable, bulky, ponderous, heavy, large, cumbersome, weighty.

ant – handy.

Unwilling (adjective)

syn – reluctant, averse, disinclined, hesitant, loath opposed.

ant – willing, eager.

Unwise (adjective)

syn – imprudent, inadvisable, injudicious, ill-advised foolish.

ant – praise, flatter.

Upbraid (verb)

syn – reproach, reprove, blame, chide, condemn, twit, taunt, scold, denounce, revile.

ant – praise, flatter

Uphold (verb)

syn – back, defend, champion, maintain, support, sustain.

ant – betray, destroy.

Uprising (noun)

syn – revolt, rebellion, strife, war, insurgency, insurrection.

ant – peace, armistice.

Upset (verb/noun)

syn – agitate, worry, disturb,

anxious, disconcert, exacerbate, demoralize, confuse, distress, enrage provoke, surprise, unsettle.

ant – calm, soothe.

Upshot (noun)

syn – conclusion, consummation, result, outcome, effect, bottom line, event.

ant – initiation, beginning.

Urbane (adjective)

syn – cultivated, genteel, sophisticated, suave, blithe, polished, cultured, well-behaved, smooth.

ant – gauche, vulgar.

Use (verb/noun)

syn – consume, employ, expend, utilize, exploit.

ant – conserve, waste.

Usual (adjective)

syn – accustomed, common, everyday, habitual, ordinary, regular, conventional, customary.

ant – unusual, occasional.

Usurp (verb)

syn – seize, arrogate, assume, confiscate, pre-empt.

ant – relinquish.

V

Vacant (adjective)

syn – empty, devoid, free, open, unoccupied, unfilled.

ant – full, occupied.

Vacillate (verb)

syn – sway, waver, fluctuate, oscillate, hestitate, be inconstant, vary.

ant – rigidity, firmness.

Vague (adjective)

syn – dim, hazy, indefinite, indistinct, obscure, indeterminate, doubtful, foggy.

ant – clear, definite.

Valid (adjective)

syn – efficacious, legal, logical, cogent, powerful, strong, well-grounded.

ant – invalid.

Vanquish (verb)

syn – conquer, overcome, overpower, overwhelm, rout, surmount, master, crush, foil, quell, defeat, subdue, outwit.

ant – surrender, capitulate, succumb.

Variety (noun)

syn – variance, assortment, diversity, multiplicity.

ant – uniformity.

Vice (noun)

syn – bestiality, corruption, perversion, immorality, villainy, wickedness.

ant – virtue.

Vicious (adjective)

syn – cruel, ferocious, fierce, savage, sinful, wicked, inhuman, nasty, barbaric, bestial, venomous.

ant – kind, generous, benevolent.

Victim (noun)

syn – butt, dupe, fool, lamb, mark, casualty, prey.

Victor (noun)

syn – conqueror, master, winner, champ, champion, subjugator.

ant – loser, vanquished.

Vehement (adjective)

syn – impetuous, violent, furious, ardent, strong, powerful, enthusiastic, zealous, passionate.

ant – tepid, subdued.

Venom (noun)

syn – poison, malignity, malice, spite, gall, rancour, bitterness, hate, virulence.

ant – benevolence.

Venture (noun/verb)

syn – bet, chance, dare, gamble, hazard, risk, stake, wager.

Veracity (noun)

syn – truth, sincerity, probity, fidelity, honesty, candour, frankness, exactness.

ant – dishonesty

Verbose (adjective)

syn – wordy, prolix, diffuse, redundant, repetitious, candour, frankness, exactness.

ant – reticent.

Versatile (adjective)

syn – changeable, variable, inconstant, fickle, erratic mercurial, capricious.

ant – rigid, fixed.

Veteran

(adjective/noun)

syn – experienced, old, seasoned, aged, expert, adept, proficient.

ant – novice.

Vexation (noun)

syn – irritation, annoyance, pique, trouble, disquiet, affliction, torment, nuisance, curse, grief, sorrow, chagrin, displeasure.

ant – delight, pleasure.

Viable (adjective)

syn – fecund, fertile, fruitful, prolific, proliferous.

ant – aborted, untenable.

Vibrate (verb)

syn – fluctuate, oscillate, sway, swing, undulate, waver, shake, totter.

ant – steady.

Vicissitude (noun)

syn – variation, mutation, revolution, change, fluctuation,

ant – stability

Victuals (noun)

syn – food, provisions, viands, sustenance, eatables.

Vie (verb)

syn – compete, contend, contest, emulate, rival.

ant – ally, associate.

View (noun/verb)

syn – belief, feeling, idea, conviction, mind, notion, opinion, position, check, inspect, study, scrutiny, aim, ambition, design, end, goal, contemplation, look, regard, panorama, prospect, scene, sight, vista, consider, eye.

Vigil (noun)

syn – watch, waking and watching, vigilance.

ant – ignore, neglect.

Vigorous (adjective)

syn – active, brisk, dynamic, energetic, effective, forceful, forcible, lusty, sturdy, powerful, active, brisk, strong.

ant – sluggish, weak, lethargic.

Vilify (verb)

syn – defame, traduce, revile, slander, libel, slur, blemish, vituperate, malign, asperse, disparage.

ant – praise, flatter.

Vim (noun)

syn – animation, bounce, brio, dash, spirit, sparkle, verve, vigor, vitality, ginger, pep, pertness.

ant – impotence, feebleness.

Vindictive (adjective)

syn – malevolent, malicious, mean, revengeful, spiteful, venomous, rancorous, resentful.

ant – forgiving.

Vintage (noun/adjective)

syn – characteristic, individual, peculiar, antiquated, dated, bygone, old fashioned, outdated, classic, classical.

ant – modern, contemporary.

Violate (verb)

syn – break, defy, disobey, flout, transgress, assault, force, rape, ravish, defile, break, breach, contravene, infringe, pollute, profane.

ant – obey, observe, uphold.

Violent (adjective)

syn – forcible, heavy, desperate, raging, stormy, rugged, tempestuous, fierce, furious, raging, tumultous.

ant – calm, gentle, moderate, passive, peaceful.

Virago (noun)

syn – shrew, fury, fishwife, harpy, termagant, vixen.

ant – saint, angel.

Virile (adjective)

syn – macho, male, manly, masculine.

ant – impotent, weak.

Virtuous (adjective)

syn – chaste, decent, modest, nice, pure, virgin, proper, moral, principled, right, righteous.

ant – villainous, immoral, wicked, vicious.

Virulence (noun)

syn – acrimony, bitterness, gall, rancor, resentment, acrimony, malevolence, venom, vindictiveness.

ant – gentleness, benevolence.

Visionary (noun/adjective)

syn – dreamer, idealist, utopian, dreamy, idealistic, chimerical, unreal, delusory, illusory, prophetic, unreal, fanciful, seer, zealot.

ant – pragmatist, realist.

Visit (noun/verb)

syn – sojourn, stay, lodge, call, look-in, chat, converse, speak, call, come by, befall, impose, inflict.

ant – depart, exit, leave.

Vista (noun)

syn – outlook, prospect, scene, perspective, sight, view.

Vital (adjective)

syn – essential, cardinal, basic, indispensable, living, alive, animate, existing, important

ant – unimportant, dead.

Vitiate (verb)

syn – abolish, abrogate, annul, cancel, annihilate, negate, void, blemish, mar, injure, flaw, damage, debase, deprave, pervert, impair.

ant – purify.

Vitriolic (adjective)

syn – acerbic, astringent, cutting, corrosive, acid, biting, caustic, mordant, sharp, stinging, trenchant, truculent.

ant – sweet, sugary, complimentary.

Vituperate (verb)

syn – abuse, assail, revile, rail against.

ant – compliment, praise, flatter.

Vivacious (adjective)

syn – lively, sprightly, brisk, animated, jocund, gay, merry, cheerful, pleasant, active, breezy.

ant – torpid.

Vocation (noun)

syn – call, summons, citation, occupation, employment, calling, business, trade.

ant – hobby.

Vogue (noun)

syn – fad, fashion, rage, custom, repute, favour, trend, mode, style.

ant – regressive.

Void (noun/adjective)

syn – abolish, abrogate, annul, cancel, negate, nullify, repeal, rescind, revoke, invalidate.

ant – establish, uphold, full, valid.

Volatile (adjective)

syn – airy, gay, gaseous, vapourific, jolly, buoyant, fickle, changeable, giddy, unsteady, wild, capricious, incoercible.

ant – stable.

Volition (noun)

syn – will, choice, preference, option, discretion, determination, purpose, elective preference.

ant – compulsion.

Volley (noun)

syn – burst, cannonade, barrage, fusillade, hail, salvo, shower, storm.

Voluminous (adjective)

syn – ample, capacious, full, wide, abundant, ample, bounteous, bountiful, copious, plentiful, substantial.

ant – scanty, slight

Voluptuous (adjective)

syn – sensual, sexual, suggestive, sensuous, hedonistic, ample, buxom, curvaceous, luscious, provocative, shapely.

ant – ascetic, saintly.

Voracious (adjective)

syn – ravenous, greedy, devouring, rapacious, hungry, is avid.

ant – sated.

Vouch (verb)

syn – attest, testify, witness, certify, affirm, endorse, guarantee, support.

Vouchsafe (verb)

syn – concede, grant, accord, allow, yield, deign, descend, stoop.

ant – refuse.

Vulgar (adjective)

syn – coarse, crude, gross, obscene, unrefined, lewd, smutty, suggestive.

ant – exquisite, polite.

Vulnerable (adjective)

syn – defenceless, exposed, untenable, powerless, weak.

ant – invincible, fortified.

Vulturine (adjective)

syn – rapacious, ravenous.

W

Wacky (adjective)

syn – absurd, crazy, daft, foolish, idiot, insane, silly, preposterous, zany, loony, nutty, lunatic, dotty, gaga, crazy, wild, zany.

ant – sensible, sane.

Wad (noun)

syn – fortune, mint, ream, ball, block, bundle, chunk, hunk, mass, plug, roll.

Wade (verb)

syn – plod, slog, slop, toil, trudge, attack, plunge, lunge, dive.

Waffle (noun/verb)

syn – ambiguity, equivocation, hedge, shuffle, prevarication, blather, jabber, prate, verbiage, wordiness.

ant – reticence, silence.

Wag (verb/noun)

syn – shake, waggle, swing, sway, jerk, droll, humorous, jester.

ant – steady, serious.

Wager (noun/verb)

syn – bet, shake, pledge, gamble, risk, wage, lay.

ant – steady, serious.

Wail (noun/verb)

syn – bay, howl, moan, yowl, ululation, bawl, blubber, weep, sob, cry.

ant – laugh, smile.

Wait (noun/verb)

syn – adjourn, defer, delay, postpone, remit, shelve, stay, suspend, waive, anticipate, abide, bide, linger, pause, stay, tarry,

ant – delay, hiatus, holdup, interval.

Waive (verb)

syn – relinquish, renounce, surrender, give up, forego, reject, desert, throw away.

ant – assert.

Wake (verb/noun)

syn – rouse, rise, awake, incite, stimulate.

ant – sleep.

Wale (noun)

syn – weal, welt, ridge, bump, lash.

Walk (verb)

syn – amble, saunter, stride, stroll, strut, swagger, waddle.

ant – run, ride.

Walkover (noun)

syn – child's play, cinch, pushover, easy victory.

Wallow (verb)

syn – flounder, roll, toss, welter, tumble, grovel.

ant – shrug.

Wan (verb/adjective)

syn – blanch, bleach, pale, pasty, sallow, waxen, ashy, careworn, drawn, haggard, cadaverous, bloodless.

ant – ruddy, flush.

Wander (verb/noun)

syn – ramble, meander, range, roam, rove, stray

ant – remain, rest.

Wane (verb/noun)

syn – decrease, diminish, abate, subside, ebb, decline, fail, sink, decay, lessening, slacken.

ant – wax, enlarge.

Wangle (verb)

syn – engineer, contrivance, guile, finesse, worm.

Want (verb/noun)

syn – beggary, destitution, pauperism, penury, poverty, privation, covet, crave, desire, wish.

ant – opulence, plenty.

Wanton (noun/adjective)

syn – baggage, hussy, jade, slattern, libertine, profligate, dissolute, uncontrolled, fast, incontinent, abandoned.

ant – chaste, pure, virginal.

War (noun/verb)

syn – battle, competition, contest, race, rivalry, strife, struggle, discord, battle, combat, duel, fight, tilt, wrestle, friction, dissension, conflict.

ant – peace, amity.

Warm (adjective/verb)

syn – lukewarm, muggy, stuffy, tepid, hot, humid, passionate.

ant – cold, chilly.

Warmth (noun)

syn – affability, amiability, geniality, pleasantness, heat, affection, cordial, genial.

ant – cold, unsympathetic.

Warp (verb/noun)

syn – twist, pervert, distort, bend, bias, prejudice, swerve, turn, wind along.

ant – straighten.

Warrant (verb/noun)

syn – guarantee, secure, assure, vouch, declare, state, attest, maintain, affirm, certify, sanction, permit, order, pass, summons.

ant – repudiate.

Waspish (adjective)

syn – slender, irritable, irascible, petulant, pettish, peevish, captious, testy, fretful, splenetic, slim, choleric.

ant – agreeable, genial.

Waste (noun/adjective/verb)

syn – destroy, ruin, idle, desolate, debris, garbage, junk, pollutants, refuse, rubbish, trash

ant – utilise.

Wave (noun/verb)

syn – billow, breaker, chop, comber, dumper, ripple, roller, shoot, surge.

Wary (adjective)

syn – alert, observant, vigilant, watchful, careful, cautious, circumspect, prudent.

ant – heedless, careless.

Wash (verb)

syn – bathe, lap, lave, bubble, splash, dampen, moisten, wet, drift, float, cleanse, scrub, rinse, launder, souse, ablution.

Wastrel (noun)

syn – prodigal, profligate, waster, spendthrift, loafer, idler, ne'er-do-well, sluggard, lazybones.

ant – industrious, hardworking.

Watch (noun/verb)

syn – guard, lookout, sentry, ward, vigil, protector, shift, spell, stint, time, tour, trick, observance, scrutiny, attend, care for, minister to, eye, beware, survey, ogle, peer, notice, stare.

Wayward (adjective)

syn – balky, contrary, difficult, impossible, capricious, erratic, fickle, undependable, flighty, ornery.

ant – complaisant, good-natured.

Weak (adjective/noun)

syn – decrepit, feeble, frail, infirm, debilitated, bony, flimsy, fragile.

ant – strong, tough.

Weaken (verb)

syn – deplete, enervate, enfeeble, exhaust, sap, spend.

ant – invigorate, energize.

Wealth (noun)

syn – assets, chattels, estate, goods, means, property, resources.

ant – poverty, scarcity, debt.

Weariness (noun)

syn – fatigue, lassitude, exhaustion, languor, languidness, boredom, tedium, monotony, sameness.

ant – refreshed, invigorated.

Weasel (noun/verb)

syn – prowler, sneak, sneaker, shuffle, equivocate, hedge.

Web (noun/verb)

syn – weave, maze, jungle, mesh, tangle, warp, catch, ensnare, entrap, tangle, trammel, trap.

Weep (verb)

syn – blubber, cry, sob, wail, whimper, grieve.

ant – laugh, rejoice.

Weird (adjective)

syn – bizarre, cranky, curious, eccentric, peculiar, odd, outlandish, eerie, uncanny, mysterious, spooky, strange.

ant – normal, usual, commonplace.

Wet (adjective/verb)

syn – damp, drench, moisten, dampen, soak, steep.

ant – dry.

Welfare (noun)

syn – aid, dole, handout,

prosperity, well-being, relief.

ant – harm.

Well-grounded (adjective)

syn – balanced, prudent, judicious, sage, sapient, sensible, cogent, solid, sound, valid.

ant – flighty, unbalanced.

Wheedle (verb)

syn – blandish, cajole, coax, charm, inveigle, importune.

Whim (noun)

syn – caprice, vagary, eccentricity, crotchet.

Whiff (noun/verb)

syn – breath, dash, hint, intimation, shade, shadow, suspicion, taste, tinge, touch, trace, whisper, nose, scent, smell, sniff.

Whimsical (adjective)

syn – capricious, freakish, odd, singular, fanciful, odd, notional, erratic, queer, quaint, curious, grotesque, outlandish.

Wield (verb)

syn – handle, flourish, manipulate, work, ply, manage, use, sway.

Wild (adjective)

syn – feral, fierce, savage, ferocious, unruly.

ant – tame, restrained.

Wilful (adjective)

syn – firm, tenacious, tough, strong-willed.

ant – timid, meek.

Wind (noun/verb)

syn – blizzard, breeze, cyclone, dust-devil, gale, hurricane, squall, storm, tempest, tornado, typhoon, whirlwind, windstorm.

Wisdom (noun)

syn – discernment, judgment, sagacity, sense, discrimination, acumens.

ant – foolishness, folly.

Wistful (adjective)

syn – dreamy, moody, nostalgic, pensive, plaintive.

ant – flippant, heedless

Wither (verb)

syn – shrivel, dry, wilt, fade, droop, wizen, waste, decay, droop, languish, wane, pine.

ant – bloom, flourish.

Withstand (verb)

syn – bear, cope, defy, endure, manage, resist, put up with, persist, fight.

ant – submit.

Woebegone (adjective)

syn – wrethed, miserable, downcast, sad, forlorn, sorrowful, crestfallen, pitiable, comfortless.

ant – joyous, happy, delighted.

Worldly (adjective)

syn – earthly, mundane, profane, secular.

ant – sacred, heavenly.

Worry (verb)

syn – agonize, brood, care, fret, bother, anxiety, solicitude.

ant – relaxed, soothe.

Wrangle (verb/noun)

syn – quarrel, bicker, spar, spat, cavil, dispute, brawl, argue, jar, tiff, contest, contention, controversy, dispute.

ant – agreement.

Wrench (verb/noun)

syn – twist, wring, sprain, strain, spanner, extort, extract, pervert, distort, unrest.

Wriggle (verb/noun)

syn – slither, squirm, wiggle, writhe, rotate, shake, vibrate.

Wrong (adjective/ noun/verb)

syn – abuse, maltreat, mistreat, oppress, persecute, inappropriate, unsuitable, incorrect, untrue.

ant – right

Wry (adjective)

syn – distorted, twisted, contorted, crooked, askew, awry, turned to one side.

ant – straight, serious.

X 

Xanthous (adjective)

syn – fair, light-complexion, fair-haired.

Xylograph (noun)

syn – wood-cut, wood-engraving.

Xylophagous (adjective)

syn – wood-eating, wood-nourished, feeding on wood.

Y 

Yank (noun/verb)

syn – jerk, lurch, snap, tug, twitch, wrench, snap.

Yap (noun/verb)

syn – squeal, yelp, yip, yawp

Yarn (noun)

syn – anecdote, fable, story, tale.

Yawn (verb)

syn – gape, open, oscillate.

Yearn (verb)

syn – hanker, long, eager, covet, hanker, crave, moon, pine.

ant – satiated.

Yea (noun/adverb)

syn – aye, yes, absolutely, agreed, gladly, unquestionably, willingly.

ant – nay.

Yell (noun/verb)

syn – call, bawl, bellow, bluster, whoop, shout, clamor, cry.

Yelp (noun/verb)

syn – squeal, yap, yip, yawp.

Yield (verb/noun)

syn – produce, permit, grant, allow, give, concede, acknowledge, afford, impart, bestow, confer, bend, relax, bow, assent, comply, obey, product, crop.

ant – resist.

Yoke (noun/verb)

syn – bond, chain, link, tie, union, servitude, couple, pair, join, associate, connect, conjoin, bracket.

ant – freedom, release.

Yokel (noun)

syn – country bumpkin, hayseed, hick, rustic, blockhead.

Youth (noun)

syn – boy, immature, lad, youngster, stripling.

ant – aged, man, adult.

Yowl (noun/verb)

syn – bay, howl, moan, wail, ululation, bawl, blubber, sob.

ant – laughter.

Z

Zany (noun)

syn – buffoon, clown, jester, droll, harlequin, punch, fool, simpleton.

ant – serious.

Zap (verb)

syn – cut off, dispatch, finish, destroy, murder, slay, knock off, liquidate, wipe out.

Zeal (noun)

syn – ardour, eagerness, alacrity, fervour, warmth, glow, devotion, feeling, energy, passion, soul, spirit, fanaticism.

ant – apathy.

Zenith (noun)

syn – summit, peak, top, pinnacle, acme, height, climax, prime, heyday.

ant – nadir, base.

Zephyr (noun)

syn – air, blast, breeze, gust, wind, blow.

Zero (noun/verb)

syn – aught, cipher, naught, nil, nought, null.

ant – infinity

Zest (noun)

syn – relish, gust, appetite, enjoyment, liking, thrill, flavour, savour, twang, pep, panache, dash, pizazz, verve, zing, zip.

ant – lethargy, exhaustion.

Zilch (noun)

syn – cipher, zero, nobody, nil, nothing, null, nonentity.

ant – zillion.

Zillion (noun)

syn – million, trillion, heap, lot, oodles, slew, wad, multiplicity.

ant – zilch

Zip (noun/verb)

syn – energy, force, steam, sprightliness, potency, power, animation, bounce, dash, spirit, verve, vigor, ginger, pertness, pep, vivacity, dart, dash, hasten, run, rush, trot, whirl, whiz.

Zone (noun)

syn – belt, girdle, girth, region, climate, circuit.

Zonked (adjective)

syn – besotted, looped, plastered, stoned, sloshed, drunk, drunken, intoxicated, inebriated.

ant – sober.

Notes